All Royalties Earned By

SPECIAL 100

Have Been Donated To

THE BAY AREA ELECTRIC RAILROAD ASSOCIATION INC.

Owner And Operator Of

THE WESTERN RAILWAY MUSEUM

Rio Vista Junction, California

and

THE ORANGE EMPIRE RAILWAY MUSEUM

Perris, California

INTERURBANS SPECIAL 100

California's Electric Railways

AN ILLUSTRATED REVIEW
BY
HARRE W. DEMORO

INTERURBAN PRESS
Glendale, California

Frontispiece:

THE WHITE FRONT cars of the Market Street Railway were essential to the success of the University of San Francisco which fancied itself as the "Streetcar College" because there were no dormitories until the 1950s. In this mid-1930s view, an outbound 5-McAllister car rattles over ex-cable car tracks past the campus and St. Ignatius Church at Fulton Street and Parker Avenue. Old-timers recall that professors in Campion Hall refused to compete with the rattles and bangs of passing streetcars and halted their lectures until the silence returned.

Waldemar Sievers

© 1986 by Harre W. Demoro

All rights reserved. No part of this book may be used or reproduced without written permission of the Publisher.

Published by
INTERURBAN PRESS
P.O. Box 6444 • Glendale, California 91205

Manufactured in the United States of America

First Printing: Fall 1986

Library of Congress Cataloging-in-Publication Data

Demoro, Harre W.
    Special 100.

    (Interurbans special : 100)
    Bibliography: p.
    Includes index.
    1. Street—railroads—California—History.   I. Title.
II. Title: Special one hundred.   III. Series.
TF724.C2D46   1986   385'.5   86-10559
ISBN 0-916374-74-2

In Memory of
CHARLES A. SMALLWOOD
1912-1986

AUTHOR, INTERURBANS SPECIAL 44

Foreword

WE SUSPECT THAT THE LATE IRA L. SWETT, who founded Interurban Press in 1943, would have approved of the circumstances that led to our decision to publish *Special 100*. We were taking a lunch break with Harre W. Demoro, who was in Glendale in March 1985 to work on Part Two of his *Key Route* with Vernon J. Sappers, a longtime Interurban Press contributor, when all of us realized a milestone was approaching. Soon the 100th Interurbans Special would be published.

Were we going to do something special to celebrate the event? That was the question posed by Demoro, who then volunteered to write a book that would celebrate the occasion. Our only rule to Demoro, who has authored or coauthored six other Interurbans Specials and was one of five coauthors of Special 26, was that the name had to include *Special 100*.

This pictorial volume on California's electric railways was the result of that conversation over hamburgers in Bengie's restaurant on Brand Boulevard, the same street that once knew the passings of Pacific Electric's Glendale-Burbank trains.

Interurban Press has come a long way since Mr. Swett founded it as a newsletter in 1943. Over the years, our late founder set most of the standards for writing and publishing works about electric railways. We think he would have been pleased at how his successors have continued his traditions and expanded in general railroad subjects, reentered the film and color slide business, and returned the company to magazine publishing by purchasing *Pacific RailNews*.

California had some of the most interesting electric railways in the world and they ranged in size from the tiny, one-car line at San Luis Obispo to the gigantic Pacific Electric Railway in Los Angeles. Fortunately, the electric railway did not disappear from California as it did in most states. Today there is a modern rail rapid transit system in the San Francisco area, a brand-new streetcar subway in San Francisco, a highly successful light rail operation in San Diego, and the promise of new electric railways in San Jose, Sacramento and Los Angeles.

We could think of no better way to celebrate the publication of our 100th Special than taking readers aboard electric traction in the Golden State.

MAC SEBREE
JIM WALKER

Acknowledgements

THIS BOOK IS A TRIBUTE TO THE EFFORTS OF dozens of amateur historians who photographed California electric railways, searched out and preserved photographic collections, and rescued records and other materials from companies going out of business, or converting to motor bus operation.

Many of the contributors are identified in photo credit lines but a number deserve special mention, including Vernon J. Sappers, Ted Wurm, John N. Harder, the late Ralph W. Demoro and the late Waldemar Sievers.

The late Francis A. Guido also deserves special mention because his magazine, *The Western Railroader*, was a treasure trove of source material.

The archives of the Bay Area Electric Railroad Association under the direction of Vernon J. Sappers and Jeffrey Wetmore also deserve credit. Items from the association are credited with the name of the photographer, when known, and BAERA.

A number of Bay Area Rapid Transit District employees were helpful in enhancing the coverage of the new rail system. They included former general managers B.R. Stokes, Lawrence Dahms and Frank Herringer, former chief engineers David G. Hammond and William Rhine, former transportation manager Alfred Wolf, former publicist Stanton W. Thies and the late William Reedy, BART Board president. Other BART officials who assisted included Joe Van Overveen, L.W. Breiner, Richard Jenevin, Malcolm Barrett, Esq., Sy Mouber, Michael Healy, Carol Asker, and P.O. Ormsbee, district secretary and semi-official historian of the project.

Municipal Railway of San Francisco officials who were helpful include retired general managers Curtis Green and John Woods, former general manager Harold Geissenheimer, retired electric transit supervisor Warren De Merritt, and James Leonard, retired information officer.

There would never have been a *Special 100* without the contributions of the late Ira L. Swett, founder of Interurban Press, and his able successors today, Mac Sebree and Jim Walker, who have kept the faith these many years. Interurban Press supplied much of the Southern California material, including views from the Ira L. Swett-Magna Collection, one of the most complete of its kind in the world.

The encouragement of Kristin A. Demoro and Jo B. Murray also is appreciated.

HARRE W. DEMORO

Contents

California's Electric Railways

STREET RAILWAY systems were already in place in many California communities by 1909, when the Glendale & Eagle Rock began service between its namesake suburban communities. This view looks east on unpaved Broadway in Glendale, with one of the California-style cars that opened the line; only horse-drawn vehicles are visible. *Craig Rasmussen Collection*

IMAGINE CALIFORNIA WHEN THE AUTOMOBILE was a curiosity, not dependable transportation, and when the few roads that existed became hopeless quagmires in winter and dust bowls in summer.

There were no gasoline stations, parking meters, shopping centers or stop signs. No monthly car payments or insurance premiums. No air pollution rules or traffic cops. No traffic jams.

Most city dwellers moved about at nine miles an hour —the pace of a horse.

Cosmopolitan San Francisco and the old Spanish era pueblo of San Jose had steam-powered trains for commuters, but generally a Californian lived close to his job and a blue collar worker might reside in company-owned quarters in the shadow of the factory where he worked. The cable car, invented in San Francisco in 1873, soon appeared in Los Angeles, Oakland and San Diego, but it was no faster than a horse. However a cable car didn't get tired like a horse, was not liable to get sick, and had no appetite for hay.

There were millions of acres of rural land surrounding most American cities, land that was too distant from downtown to be useful as residential suburbs. America was still largely an agricultural nation and most of its rural population was isolated from the amenities of city life. Train travel was too expensive and railroad schedules infrequent. A horse and buggy, for the farmer who could afford one, was uncomfortable and slow.

Two inventions would dramatically change this leisurely, if sometimes frustrating, lifestyle: One was the automobile, the other the electric railway. Both appeared on the American scene at about the same time—in the decade before the beginning of the 20th century.

The automobile developed slowly. It needed a network of highways, service stations and parking garages, and the governmental institutions to provide these necessities. Electric railways were much easier to develop, and could be nurtured by the private enterprise framework already in place. Generally, they were easier and quicker to build than steam railroads, a factor that delighted stock and bond houses accustomed to transportation and utility financing.

The electric railway had several inventors but the man who perfected the technology was a young Naval Academy graduate, Frank Julian Sprague. His first system began operation in 1888 in Richmond, Virginia, and the equipment spread quickly to the rest of the country, with California quickly becoming one of the major centers of the electric railway.

There had been several pre-Sprague systems in California, none of them successful. Two examples were a line using electric locomotives pulling trailers, which operated in Los Angeles in 1888 and 1889, and an enterprise in San Jose that experimented with cars powered by a conduit beneath the street.

By 1891, there were at least six California cities with reliable electric street railways: Sacramento, San Jose, Los Angeles, Santa Cruz, Oakland and San Francisco.

Within 20 years, there were electric street railways in many other California cities, including Eureka, Chico, Marysville, Yuba City, Stockton, Fresno, Bakersfield, Monterey, Pacific Grove and Santa Barbara.

Some cities of significant size and influence had streetcar service provided by the system in an adjacent community. For example, Berkeley, San Leandro, Hayward, Piedmont and Alameda were served by the Oakland-based Key System. In Southern California, the Pacific Electric provided streetcar service for Pasadena, Long Beach, San Pedro, Glendale and several cities in the San Bernardino area. The Sacramento Northern ran streetcars in Sacramento, Marysville, Yuba City and Chico, and the Central California Traction ran streetcars in Sacramento and Stockton.

LINES BETWEEN CITIES

An important milestone was reached in 1892, when the Oakland, San Leandro & Hayward's Electric Railway began operating between its namesake cities. For a time this was the longest electric railroad in the world, and its success showed that electric traction was useful for more than local service within a city. The Hayward line was never more than a slow trolley route but there were to be many electric railways that would operate at high speeds over considerable distances between cities.

The opening of the Pasadena & Los Angeles Electric Railway in 1895 was the beginning of the Pacific Electric Railway, the largest interurban system in the world. PE tracks extended from Redlands on the east to Santa Monica on the western Pacific shore, and from Mount Lowe and San Fernando on the north to Balboa on the sunny southwest coast of the basin. Southern Pacific began buying Los Angeles interurban lines early in the

12, 1891.

| on the Oak-
'ransit Road,
0 feet along
into sections.
mishap occur
ven section it
that section.
I continue to
just as usual.
ment at the
the trolley
and its exact
particular sec-
tely repaired.
ystem if an
olley wire ia
te and all the
a cable road
n, because in
m the elec-
trolley wire.
mportance in
on this road.
bel the cars is
ire, while an-
t which lights
trolley ceases
a are not ex-

Sprague, the
on the Oak-
it road, gave
icerning his
ie course of
development
aled in the
id. In 1886 a
omprised all
on, and this
in the world,
olit tube, the
r carriage on
rail, or by a
. There was
ent plans, but
electricity, in
could propel
en were dis-
, car builders
only hopeful,
as opened for
m a road at
ented condi-
roadbed and
d, which, if
mark a new
ectrical rail-
s, while not
rkable, were
le, not only
to street-car
lectrical and

n to twelve
grade of 10
curves of 7 |

with reference to the method of supplying the current. This will undoubtedly be by the overhead single conductor underneath contact system, with rail and tunnel return, despite the criticisms of what is properly known as the overhead wire-system, which is the necessary street develop-ment, with many limitations, of the under-neath plan."

ON A BROOMSTICK TRAIN.

The Car That Holmes Says Is Plainly Moved by Witches.

The First Day of Regular Traffic Passes Without Disaster, Hitch or Delay of Any Kind.

It was just 5:35 o'clock this morning when the pioneer regular service car came swinging out from the big carhouse at the corner of Forty-seventh and Grove streets, and as it turned and sped on toward Oak-land with all the regularity of a well-tried machine Superintendent Coleman and his men braced up to meet the probable dis-asters of the first day's running. Such a time is always eventful in the history of a new line, especially when the motive power is electricity, for there are many possibilities in the shape of breaks, non-working of switches and curves, failure of current, and so on, while for a car or two to get off the track on the first day of service is expected as an almost certain event. Over at the engine house, though, there seemed little indication of trouble. The steady hum of machinery, the constant glowing of the indicating lights and the ceaseless revolutions of the big wheels showed that everything was working without a hitch, and the engineer, as he stood with a piece of waste in each hand, smiled as he gazed down at the motive-making power and in response to a ques-tion said: "We're not going to have any-thing go wrong here."

His assurance might well have been echoed from without, for the first car rattled down to Oakland and back without any trouble at all and then, as at regular intervals the other cars were brought out and put in service, every one connected with the road began to feel su-premely happy, for the morning was wear-

| is the power
next block wi
so on," and a
feeling himsel
back with a si
At the powe
stopped to wa
also the compl
etc., as the ca
ing at the obli
one could not
Wendell Holi
Monthly on wi
train," for h
electric cars
spirits of witc
being the pole
The witch th
But you can c
And in conr
noticeable thi
Berkeley line
have traveled
roads. It is ti
noise in transi
noticeable on
roads for insta
And now, as
day and ton
after no sche
to, though a
about twenty
leave the c
though, and
Berkeley at 6
Oakland at 12
through trip t
carhouse. O
pected that t
established, ar
ten minutes du
time occupied
just eighty mi

NAT

Growing Slov

More Than (
Debt Wipe
United Sta

WASHINGTON
reau has issue
of the world,
the debts of f
the sinking fur |

OAKLAND'S FIRST streetcar was treated almost with amaze-ment by the *Oakland Tribune*, which reported on May 12, 1891, that the Oakland-Berkeley line opened without incident. "We're not going to have anything go wrong here," the power house engineer assured the reporter. *Oakland Tribune*

20th century and formed the second company to be named Pacific Electric in 1911. By the 1920s, PE was running 2,160 trains a day over more than 1,000 miles of track.

The Sacramento Northern Railway, built by several predecessor companies from 1906 to 1913 between a terminal on San Francisco Bay and Chico in the upper Sacramento Valley, had a main line 183 miles long and another 65 miles of branches. Trains often reached 60 miles an hour as they sped over the flat delta and agricul-tural lands toward the capital city of Sacramento, and some schedules offered dining and parlor car service.

Another fast line, the San Francisco & Napa Valley, connected with the Monticello steamers from San Fran-cisco and ran over a 41.6-mile electrified line to Calistoga in the wine and geyser country. There were the high-speed cars of the Central California Traction Co.'s inter-urban line between Stockton, Lodi and Sacramento, the fast Tidewater Southern trains running from Stockton to Modesto, and the Petaluma & Santa Rosa cars that carried passengers and eggs to the paddlewheel steamer landing at Petaluma.

In San Diego, the interurbans went north to La Jolla and south to National City, Chula Vista and Otay. The Visalia Electric operated through the lemon groves around Exeter, and the Peninsular Railway linked San Jose with Los Gatos, Los Altos and Palo Alto.

The three largest California streetcar systems were in Los Angeles, Oakland and San Francisco. In 1931, for example, the Los Angeles Railway Corporation operated 1,226 narrow-gauged streetcars over 403 miles of track; Oakland's Key System, then operating as East Bay Street Railways Ltd., had about 350 streetcars running on 180 miles of track; San Francisco had two electric street rail-way systems, the city-owned Municipal Railway with 234 cars and 78 miles of track, and the privately owned Market Street Railway Company, which had 725 electric cars on 270 miles of track.

These figures do not include San Francisco's cable system, then under two ownerships, or the 213 suburban electric cars in Marin County and the Oakland area, the Key System's 129 interurban cars, or the Pacific Electric roster, which included a considerable number of street-cars in addition to its interurban cars. PE's passenger car fleet totaled 777 cars in 1931.

An offshoot of streetcar and interurban technology was the suburban commuter railroad that used self-propelled electric passenger coaches. There were two in California, both in the San Francisco Bay Area.

The first was the pioneering North Shore in Marin County, which originally was a narrow-gauged railroad running between Sausalito and the redwood forests on the north coast. John Martin and Eugene de Sabla, who were prominent in hydroelectric power development, electrified the southern section of the North Shore in 1903, using standard-gauged passenger cars similar to those designed for steam trains, but propelled by electricity. This was the first electrified commuter railroad of its type in the United States and it set the design patterns for the electrification of Grand Central Terminal in New York and the first New York "Interborough" subway. The Northwestern Pacific took over the NS in 1907; the service had 66 cars on 40 miles of electrified track in 1931.

The second California electrified suburban railway was the Southern Pacific's network in Oakland, Alameda and Berkeley completed between 1911 and 1915; by 1931 SP was running 147 cars on 119 miles of East Bay track.

SP electrified its steam commuter lines and built several new electrified lines to meet the competition from the Key System, which had constructed an interurban railway in Oakland, Berkeley and Piedmont between 1903 and 1911, and had 129 cars on 60 miles of track in 1931. SP and Key trains fought for business between the East Bay and San Francisco, using ferries for the connection to the city. These operations were separate from Key's extensive local streetcar network.

RAILWAY — UTILITY CONNECTIONS

The ownership of California electric railways did not follow the usual pattern often found elsewhere. For example, in many areas, including the Pacific Northwest and Midwest, many street railways and interurbans were owned by electric light companies. There was a good reason for this: In the early days there were few electric appliances in the home, and factories were not major consumers of electricity. As a result, power stations ran streetcars during the daytime and supplied electricity for electric lights at night.

In California, only three companies were directly in the street railway business for any length of time, the Pacific Gas and Electric Company, Southern California Edison Company and San Joaquin Light and Power Corporation. The Sacramento Electric Power & Light Company bought Sacramento's street railways in 1892 and in 1896 a successor electric company took over the streetcars and ran them until Pacific Gas & Electric appeared in 1906 and ran them until 1943. For many years cars in Sacramento had the same "P G and E" emblem homeowners found on their monthly electric bills. In Santa Barbara, the streetcar system was bought in 1902 by

United Electric Gas & Power Co., which soon was acquired by Southern California Edison, which ran the cars until the system was abandoned in 1929. The San Joaquin company, which came under PG&E control in the 1930s, owned the Bakersfield & Kern Electric Railway from 1910 to 1933.

There were cases of indirect power utility-electric railway involvement in California.

PG&E executives were instrumental in the electrification of the North Shore (later Northwestern Pacific) Railroad in Marin County in 1902-03. Some of the same investors were active in the promotion of the Northern Electric (Sacramento Northern), the Nevada County Traction and Santa Cruz street railway. Financiers active in Great Western Power Company also were influential in the development of the Central California Traction Company and the Oakland, Antioch & Eastern (Sacramento Northern). Henry Huntington had his hand in Southern California Edison Company as well as the original Pacific Electric and the Los Angeles Railway.

In San Diego, the Spreckels interests developed both the San Diego Electric Railway and the San Diego Gas & Electric, but the companies were kept separate. There were similar indirect links with the United Railroads of San Francisco and in Oakland, where electric utility interests affiliated with F.M. (Borax) Smith unsuccessfully tried to create a huge utility empire of railroads, waterfront wharves, real estate and electric railways.

PRIVATE OWNERSHIP

A considerable number of traction companies were financed by public stock and bond promotions, although in later years most small investors lost their money because of the industry's poor earnings.

A few financial syndicates were active in the early days. Smith in Oakland, Piedmont and Berkeley even called his investment group "Syndicate Railways" for a time. A Baltimore financial group controlled the United Railroads of San Francisco which, after it was reorganized as the Market Street Railway in 1921, was in the hands of the Byllesby management group for some years. Byllesby was involved in various kinds of utility operations.

A lot of diehard San Franciscans favored the city-owned cars because the Market Street Railway, they complained, was controlled by "Eastern Capitalists."

Several financial syndicates were involved in Los Angeles interurban projects, including the Sherman-Clark team that built the Los Angeles Pacific and the first Pasadena line. The Northern Electric, Oakland, Antioch

& Eastern (Sacramento Northern) and Central California Traction all benefited to some extent by their access to San Francisco Jewish money. Indeed, the Northern Electric's troubles almost destroyed the Sloss fortune which, with Lilienthal family money, was involved in financing the Pacific Gas and Electric Co. Jewish banker Isaias W. Hellman sold the first bonds for Henry Huntington's original Pacific Electric in 1901 and was on the PE's first board of directors. He was previously involved in the original Market Street Railway in San Francisco.

Several electric railways owned floating equipment. Key System, Southern Pacific and North Shore (Northwestern Pacific) all owned ferryboats that took electric commuter train passengers to San Francisco. The Sacramento Northern had a ferry that carried an entire train across the river near Pittsburg and the Petaluma & Santa Rosa owned river steamers that connected with its electric trains at Petaluma. The San Francisco & Napa Valley did not own a ferry but depended almost entirely on the connecting steamers at Vallejo. The ferry was so important that the interurban gave up a week after the steamers quit in 1937.

A major financial influence in California were steam railroads which moved early into the electric railway field, perhaps on a scale unequaled elsewhere in the United States, except for the New England holdings of the New York, New Haven & Hartford.

Besides owning the PE and the Oakland suburban lines, the Southern Pacific operated Stockton Electric, Visalia Electric, Fresno Traction, Peninsular Railway and San Jose Railroads. From 1906-1929, SP and the Atchison, Topeka & Santa Fe owned the Northwestern Pacific, and after 1929 NWP was wholly owned by SP. Through NWP, SP gained control of the Petaluma & Santa Rosa in 1932. With Santa Fe and Western Pacific, the SP owned a third interest in the Central California Traction.

Western Pacific (which was merged into the Union Pacific in 1982) was especially interested in electric railways because, as the last transcontinental to reach California, it had few branch lines of its own to generate freight business. WP gained control of the Sacramento Northern lines north of Sacramento and in the Vacaville area in 1921 and merged those operations into the San Francisco-Sacramento Railroad (Oakland-Sacramento) in 1929, to create the 183-mile Sacramento Northern Railway. WP also bought the Tidewater Southern in 1917.

WP invested heavily in new electric locomotives for the Sacramento Northern and Tidewater Southern and both companies continued to haul freight electrically after the SN abandoned mainline passenger service in

STEEPLE CAB electric locomotives were common on California roads. Wooden Tidewater Southern 100 was built by the Central California Traction in 1912 and scrapped in 1948.

L. L. Bonney

1940 and 1941 and Tidewater Southern got out of the passenger business in 1932. SN had a modest amount of electric operation in the Marysville-Yuba City area as late as 1965 and the Tidewater Southern remained electric until 1948 over a small portion of the line in Modesto.

The Central California Traction Company abandoned mainline passenger service in 1933, but continued to haul freight electrically until 1946. The Petaluma & Santa Rosa retained its electric locomotives until 1947, 15 years after passenger operations ceased, and the Visalia Electric, which got out of the passenger business in 1924, finally turned off the electricity in 1944.

In most cases, freight operation continued under diesel power after the electricity was shut off. Portions of the Sacramento Northern have been merged into its parent, the Union Pacific, and the Traction Company and Visalia Electric function as dieselized freight feeders for their parent railroads.

The Petaluma & Santa Rosa finally gave up entirely in 1984 but major portions of the Pacific Electric have been amalgamated into Southern Pacific's Los Angeles freight network. A portion of the Key System has survived as the Oakland Terminal, a dieselized freight feeder to its parents, the Santa Fe and Union Pacific.

After 1937, a portion of the Napa Valley line remained electrified for freight until diesels took over the surviving section around Vallejo in 1942. A small amount of track was retained in 1956 for freight switching at the Mare Island Naval Shipyard in Vallejo.

STANDARDIZATION

There was a considerable amount of standardization among electric railways in California but there also were subtle differences due to varied operating conditions and the fact that the basic statewide network developed over 25 years and technological improvements had an impact.

All electric railways except the Los Angeles Railway and two isolated examples on the California coast ultimately settled on the standard 4-foot, 8½-inch gauge used by steam railroads. The 42-inch LARY gauge was a holdover from cable cars. The single electric car operated at San Luis Obispo ran over the 3-foot-gauge Pacific Coast Railroad steam line, and the Watsonville Transportation Co., which only had two electric railway cars, used 3-foot gauge so it could interchange freight cars with the steam-operated Pajaro Valley Consolidated Railroad.

The electrical systems were less standardized. Street railways used the standard 600-volt (sometimes rated at 550 volts) direct-current system that evolved from Sprague's work in Richmond, Virginia. Most early interurban lines also used this voltage which made it simple for the intercity cars to run over local streetcar lines in cities. The majority of interurban stock was narrower and shorter than necessary to negotiate sharp streetcar curves.

Most of the Pacific Electric was built to 600 volts as were the Sacramento Northern lines north of Sacramento and an early SN branch line in the Vacaville area. The Key System, North Shore (Northwestern Pacific), Peninsular Railway, Petaluma & Santa Rosa and the San Diego area interurbans were 600 volts.

Although the 600-volt system was suitable for city operation it was less than ideal for lines over long distances. Because expensive electrical substations had to be located at frequent intervals on 600-volt interurban lines, efforts began around 1900 to develop better electrical power supplies.

For a brief time, the Westinghouse Electric & Manufacturing Company offered an alternating current system that avoided the power loss but resulted in sluggish performance by the cars. Alternating current systems were installed on two California interurbans, the San Francisco & Napa Valley, which started to use 750 volts but soon raised the voltage to 3,300, the AC voltage also adopted by the Visalia Electric.

The General Electric Company was still under the influence of Thomas A. Edison, who championed direct current. GE developed a highly reliable 1,200-volt direct-current system. There is some evidence that the first line to choose the GE 1,200-volt equipment was the Central California Traction Company in 1907, but it was not the first to actually use the system. That honor fell to the Indianapolis & Louisville Traction Company in Indiana, which finished its line between Seymour and Sellersburg shortly before the Traction Company opened its Stockton-Lodi line that same year.

The 1,200-volt system was highly successful because it sharply reduced the number of substations required for 600-volt operations while avoiding the control and weight problems of alternating current. The 1,200-volt and similar 1,500-volt equipment introduced later soon became the standard for long-distance interurban lines.

The economy of high-voltage DC was demonstrated by the Oakland, Antioch & Eastern Railway, which adopted 1,200 volts for its Oakland-Sacramento line (which later became part of the Sacramento Northern). Only five substations were required for the 76-mile line completed in 1913. OA&E cars had switches also allowing them to operate at full speed on 600 volts and ran at this voltage to the Key System ferry pier in Oakland. The train had to be stopped to change the voltage setting so in Sacramento the OA&E ran at half speed, with the cars still set for 1,200 volts, while drawing 600 volts from the PG&E streetcar system and the Northern Electric.

The Tidewater Southern was built as a 1,200-volt road and Pacific Electric used 1,200 volts on most of its 63-mile San Bernardino line opened in 1914. Like the OA&E, PE had cars that could easily change voltage, and some dual-voltage PE cars could change while in motion.

The spring-raised trolley pole was used by most California electric railways to collect electrical power but this method was far from a universal practice.

The North Shore Railroad (Northwestern Pacific) used an electrically charged third rail laid alongside the running rail. A tongue-like piece of metal mounted on the car slid on the top of the electric rail. The Northern Electric (Sacramento Northern) had the same type of electric third rail on its lines north of Sacramento, except where cars ran in city streets an overhead pole trolley was necessary. This same dual system was used by the NE on its Vacaville area line. On the Central California Traction, the shoe rubbed on the bottom of the third rail, and CCT passenger cars used pole trolley in city streets.

The Oakland, Antioch & Eastern used a pantograph trolley on the Key System, then switched to trolley poles for the run from Oakland to Sacramento. When the OA&E became part of the Sacramento Northern, its cars also were fitted with third rail shoes so they could operate on the former Northern Electric lines.

The pantograph first appeared in California in 1903 on

the Key System's interurban cars. It was adopted also by the two AC roads, the San Francisco & Napa Valley and the Visalia Electric. San Francisco's "light rail cars" and similar cars on the new San Diego line use modern versions of pantographs, as will cars on order in 1985 for new light rail lines in San Jose and Sacramento. Some old San Diego and Oakland streetcars also had pantographs. The Napa Valley and Pacific Electric briefly tested bow-type trolleys that were once popular in Europe.

Pantographs also were used by SP on its East Bay suburban trains. When the Key System and SP shared track on the Bay Bridge starting in 1939, SP collected 1,200 volts with pantographs and Key lowered its pantographs on the joint track and collected 600 volts with third rail shoes.

The Central California Traction Co. equipped its passenger and freight motors with pantographs as well as third rail shoes and pole trolleys in the early days. However, for most of its history of electric operation, the Traction Co. used third rail shoes and pole trolleys on passenger and freight motor cars. Pantographs appeared on freight motors in the last years of electric operations, in addition to third rail shoes and a pole trolley.

There was considerable variety on Sacramento Northern freight locomotives. Some had poles and third rail shoes, others had third rail shoes, poles and pantographs, and some had pantographs and pole trolleys but no third rail equipment.

Cars for Mild Climates

Because of the mild climate—no California electric railway had to contend with snow and ice, except in unusual circumstances—streetcars and interurbans in the Golden State were often much different from those of other systems.

The practice of having open and closed sections was popularized by San Francisco cable car designers and the concept was transferred to electric traction. A car with an enclosed center section and open end sections was generally known as the "California Type" because the design first appeared on the California Street Cable Railroad in San Francisco about 1895.

Cars with open and closed sections were adopted almost universally by California streetcar operators. Moreover, a considerable number were constructed for high-speed interurban lines. The Pacific Electric and its predecessors had hundreds of interurbans with open sections; some of them continued running into the 1930s. The San Francisco & Napa Valley also had open-closed

interurbans and some San Diego cars lacked windows so the mild Southern California climate could be enjoyed.

Los Angeles Transit Lines, successor to Los Angeles Railway, ran streetcars with open end sections into the 1950s.

Indeed, the variety of California electric railway car designs seemed endless.

Pacific Electric's fleet ranged from tiny wooden streetcars to heavy steel interurban cars. Sacramento Northern owned a series of ornate interurban cars built by the Niles Car & Manufacturing Co., and in the interurban company shops, that were among the most graceful appearing in the industry. Similar cars were acquired from Niles by the San Francisco & Napa Valley.

Key System's interurban fleet ranged from gracefully appearing wooden interurbans with decorations etched into windows to utilitarian-appearing steel center-door cars and streamlined trains that were hinged in the center to negotiate curves.

The Market Street Railway built about 250 cars in its own shops with low platforms close to the street for fast loading and unloading. Many of these cars had leather seats, but the typical California streetcar seat was wooden or upholstered in stiff rattan.

Interurbans tended to be fancier than city cars, often having leather or plush seats. Cars operating over long distances had lavatories and wash basins. City streetcars had melodic gongs, or bells, but interurban cars usually had horns or whistles as well as air-operated bells. The Sacramento Northern used air whistles within city limits and sharp-sounding air horns in the country, mostly because of municipal ordinances regulating noise.

Most companies believed that their operating conditions were unique and bought standard electrical and mechanical components but used carbodies specifically designed for their own use. There was often not even standardization within one company. Typically, a traction line would have large groups of cars that differed from one another.

Among the few standardized cars popular in California were the Hedley-Doyle Car, the Birney Safety Car and the PCC Car.

The Hedley-Doyle Car was a dragon-shaped streetcar designed to operate in New York. Its principal feature was its low center step, which earned it the name "Hobbleskirt Car" because women wearing the restrictive skirt popular at the time could board the cars with ease. But the cars were slow and ungainly—and ugly. Southern Pacific bought 35 in 1913 and assigned them to Pacific Electric, San Jose Railroads, Stockton Electric and Fresno Traction. They were all gone by the mid-1930s.

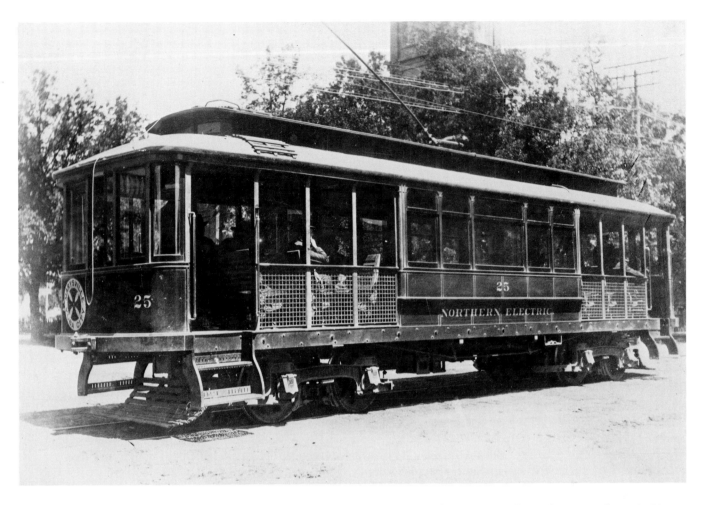

A DESIGN THAT began in Los Angeles on the Los Angeles Railway and Pacific Electric also appeared on the Key System and the Northern Electric, a predecessor of the Sacramento Northern. NE bought its "Huntington Standards" for streetcar service in the Sacramento Valley and NE 25 is shown in Marysville-Yuba City service shortly after it was built by the St. Louis Car Company in 1906. The cars later were enclosed and rebuilt for suburban service. *Harre W. Demoro Collection*

The Birney Safety Car was more successful. This was a two-axle car that could be operated by one man. "Safety devices" stopped the car if the motorman was disabled or the door was open. The cars, which tended to gallop along because they only had four wheels, were used in Bakersfield, Chico, Marysville, Fresno, Glendale (Glendale & Montrose Railway), Los Angeles (LARY's were narrow gauge, PE's standard), Oakland, Sacramento (both by PG&E and SN), San Diego, San Jose (both by San Jose Railroads and Peninsular), Santa Barbara, Santa Cruz and Stockton. The cars moved around within California, with most of SN's Birneys being built for San Diego. SP transferred its Birneys between its streetcar properties on several occasions.

Pacific Gas & Electric (Sacramento), Fresno Traction and Glendale & Montrose had double-truck versions (with four axles) of the Birney design; the Fresno cars later were sold to Pacific Electric and the Central California Traction and two of the three Glendale & Montrose cars were acquired by the San Diego Electric Railway.

Sacramento Northern was the last to run Birneys in California, with the final trip occurring on December 15, 1947, in Chico.

The PCC Car was a highly standardized streetcar developed by the transit industry in the 1930s as an unsuccessful attempt to revive the street railway which, by then, was in an irreversible decline. PCC cars looked

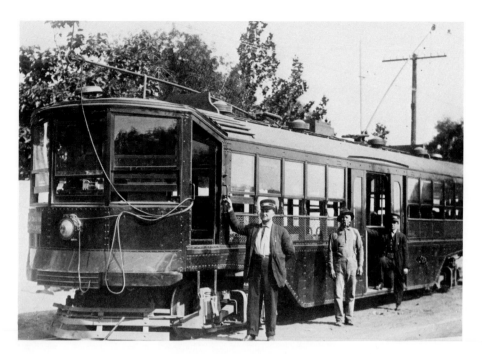

AMONG THE STANDARD streetcar designs found in California was the strange-looking Hedley-Doyle Stepless Car, also known as a Hobbleskirt Car or a Dragon. This is one of four cars that Southern Pacific bought in 1913 from J. G. Brill Company for Fresno Traction Company. SP also acquired Dragons for its Pacific Electric, San Jose Railroads and Stockton Electric subsidiaries.

Charles A. Smallwood Collection

somewhat like the buses they were supposed to challenge, but they rode whisper-like on rubber-cushioned wheels and springs and had rapid and smooth acceleration and braking.

San Diego Electric Railway and Los Angeles Railway were quick to try the PCC Car, with both systems receiving new PCCs in 1937-38, shortly after they were introduced. Ultimately, LARY and its successor, Los Angeles Transit Lines, had 165 PCC cars and San Diego, 28.

San Francisco bought five experimental modern cars in 1939 for testing and the Pacific Electric acquired 30 double-ended PCC cars that could be coupled into trains in 1940. After World War II, the San Francisco Municipal Railway amassed a fleet of 116 PCC cars, but only 35 were acquired brand new. The rest came from St. Louis and Toronto, and the Toronto cars had first operated in Kansas City.

PCC cars ran in San Diego until that system was abandoned in 1949 and most of its PCCs were sold to El Paso City Lines. Pacific Electric's PCC fleet was idled in 1955 when the Glendale-Burbank Line was discontinued and the cars ultimately were sold to a railroad in Argentina. The other Los Angeles cars ran until a transit authority replaced streetcars with buses in 1963. Some of the PCCs were sold to two cities in Egypt. San Francisco's PCC cars ran until 1982 when new light rail cars took over all surface and subway routes. But about 50 are in storage and may run again on a proposed new waterfront line.

The Pacific Electric and Los Angeles Railway systems had a profound impact on electric railway car design early in the century because their vast scale encouraged a great degree of standardization. The "Huntington Standard" style with open ends, enclosed center and five-window front developed by the Los Angeles properties also appeared on the Northern Electric (Sacramento Northern) and East Shore & Suburban (Key System). LARY's Huntington Standards were the most durable. The design was in use on LARY and its successor from 1902-1952. Also, PE's 800-class interurban design was copied by the Napa Valley and Central California Traction.

Several electric railways had special cars fitted out for excursions or, in the case of the Sacramento Northern, to offer comforts usually found on mainline railroads.

The SN had four parlor-observation cars, the *Bidwell, Sacramento, Moraga* and *Alabama*, which offered dining service until the early 1930s along the route from the Key System Pier in Oakland and Sacramento and Chico. Some SN trains had names, like *Comet, Meteor, Sacramento Valley Limited* and *Steamer Special.*

The Sacramento Northern was a strong competitor against Southern Pacific steam trains for traffic between San Francisco and the state capital at Sacramento.

The *Alabama* was an especially interesting car, having been built in 1905 as the private car of the Pacific Electric's Henry Huntington, who kept the car for himself after the Great Merger of 1911 put him out of the interurban picture. The car saw little use after the amalgamation and was sold in 1921 to the Sacramento Northern Railroad. The elegant car was destroyed at Dozier, 30 miles south of Sacramento, by a fire caused by a short circuit in a coffee maker in 1931.

No other Northern California interurban had parlor-observation cars but several street railways had special excursion equipment and San Francisco boasted a streetcar reserved for its schoolchildren. This car, named *San Francisco*, was made available for free to schools for outings and field trips.

Pacific Electric and its predecessors had at least 20 special cars and both the interurban company and private firms ran tours and special excursions to tout the beauties of Southern California. One early car reflected the early Spanish influence of the region with its name, *El Viento* (the Wind). Car 1299 was built by PE in 1928-29 from a former Portland electric car into a company officers' car and parlor car. Late in its long career the 1299 carried regular paying passengers to Newport Beach as the "Commodore" until June 30, 1950. This was the last named electric car service in the west.

Most California interurbans and streetcar systems carried mail. San Francisco, Oakland and Los Angeles were among operators in the state of railway post office service in which mail was sorted en route. Pacific Electric had an extensive fleet of "box motors" for less-than-carload freight and railway post office service. Box motor service was discontinued in favor of trucks in 1952; the last railway post office service on a U.S. electric railway operated on PE between Los Angeles and San Bernardino until 1949.

CALIFORNIA CARBUILDERS

Because California was a considerable distance from midwest and eastern railway carbuilders, which tended to be in those areas because of the great number of electric railways east of Chicago, many electric railways in the Golden State built their own streetcars and interurbans, or bought them from local firms. This saved the cost of shipping by rail and also aided the local economy. In most cases, the cars turned out by the operating companies and local builders were the equal of products sold by established manufacturers outside the state, and in some cases they probably were better.

In the San Francisco area, both the Key System and Market Street Railway (and its predecessor United Railroads) built hundreds of cars. Key System's huge shops at Emeryville was actually a railway factory capable of

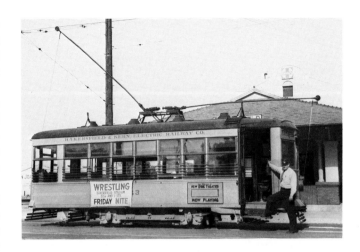

BAKERSFIELD BIRNEY 23 was built for Santa Cruz and was later sold to Halifax, Nova Scotia. *Above, George Henderson; below, Harre W. Demoro*

building interurban cars as well as streetcars and able to repair locomotives and ferryboat machinery.

The Los Angeles Railway also built cars and Pacific Electric's huge Torrance Shops rebuilt hundreds of cars but did not build passenger cars from scratch. Some of the rebuilding done at Torrance and at other PE shops was so thorough it could be considered new construction. PE built a number of heavy electric freight locomotives at Torrance using steel fabricated at a nearby shipyard. A PE

PACIFIC ELECTRIC'S PCC cars were the first constructed for multiple-unit train operation and were delivered by Pullman-Standard in 1940. The 30 double-ended cars spent most of their careers on the busy Glendale-Burbank line operating out of Subway Terminal until the line was converted to bus in 1955.

predecessor, the Los Angeles & Redondo, built inter-urban cars.

San Diego Electric also constructed streetcars and the Sacramento system built cars for its trackage as well as for Bakersfield, San Jose, Palo Alto and Santa Cruz. Sacramento Northern predecessor Northern Electric Railway built six ornate interurban cars at Chico that were duplicates of wooden cars the NE previously had bought from Niles Car & Manufacturing Company. Likewise, the North Shore (NWP) at Sausalito built wooden electric cars for its third rail lines that were exact duplicates of rolling stock supplied at the same time by the St. Louis Car Company.

Locally, there were several carbuilders in the San Francisco area that did a thriving business supplying streetcars and interurbans.

The most prolific were the Hammond and Holman companies in San Francisco, which were independent during most of their histories but apparently merged after the San Francisco fire in 1906. Holman built interurban cars for several roads including the Oakland, Antioch & Eastern and Central California Traction and dozens of streetcars. It got into financial trouble in 1912 trying to build the first steel streetcars for the new San Francisco Municipal Railway and went out of business after building 20 cars. The Union Iron Works Shipyard, later Bethlehem Steel, took over the contract and delivered the final 23 in the order in 1913. The shipyard also built 20 Municipal cars in 1923.

Carter Brothers, which was founded in 1872 at Sausalito but moved to Newark a few years later, is mostly known for railroad, horse and cable cars. But before the firm went out of business about 1903 it built cars for the Oakland, San Leandro & Hayward's and San Francisco's Metropolitan Railway and supplied the first electric cars for Sacramento. A steam coach it delivered in the mid-1890s to the California Railway in Oakland was electrified as an overhead trolley maintenance car in 1915 by Key System and a similar Carter product delivered to the California Railway was electrified in the 1890s.

Hall-Scott, a Berkeley firm better known for manufacturing aircraft and bus engines and gasoline-driven railway cars, built eight steel interurban cars for the Oakland, Antioch & Eastern. A. Meister in Sacramento built one streetcar for the San Francisco Municipal Railway. Stockton Combine, Harvester & Agricultural Works built a number of streetcars in the 1890s for companies in Oakland, Portland, Tacoma and Salem, Oregon. The company also was known as Holt Brothers and was involved in the early development of tractors and other agricultural machinery.

The big eastern and midwestern manufacturers did build hundreds of electric railway cars for California lines.

St. Louis Car Company, one of the biggest, supplied at least 500 cars over the years to the Pacific Electric and its predecessors. These cars ranged in size and assignment from 110 of the highly successful "Hollywood" steel center-door cars (600 and 700 type and later 5050 type) delivered between 1922 and 1928, to the 44 950-class cars built for predecessor Los Angeles Pacific which were completed in 1907 for the heavily traveled lines to Santa Monica.

Most electric railways bought cars in small batches. An order for more than 50 cars was unusual because companies were not often well financed. Also, cars were bought as lines were built and expanded.

St. Louis Car Company received the largest order from a traditional California electric railway in 1907 when the United Railroads bought 200 streetcars (URR 1550-1749). The cars were delivered in 1906-07 to help San Francisco rebuild after the Great Fire of April 18, 1906. That order was not exceeded in size in California until the Bay Area Rapid Transit (BART) District ordered 250 cars (150 with cabs, 100 without cabs) from Rohr Industries Inc., of Chula Vista near San Diego, in 1969. Although BART ultimately acquired 450 cars following the same design from Rohr, the second 200 were bought in two batches of 100 each and legally were not part of the 1969 purchase.

The Philadelphia-based J.G. Brill Company, the largest carbuilder in the world, also was a major supplier of California electric lines, but most of that production was from its St. Louis subsidiary, the American Car Company, which was nearest the West Coast market.

Examples of American Car Company products were 65 streetcars for the United Railroads in 1914 (201-265) that were to be the pattern for home-built cars, two series of almost identical 95 lightweight streetcars for the Key System in Oakland in 1923 and 1926 (cars 900-994), and 50 slightly larger cars of the same general design for San Diego Electric Railway (the 400-449) in 1923. American-built cars could be found on the Peninsular Railway, Pacific Electric, Los Angeles Railway, PG&E (Sacramento), Central California Traction and Visalia Electric, among others.

Products from other Brill subsidiaries were uncommon in California. The Wason Manufacturing Company of Springfield, Massachusetts, supplied four interurban cars (the 1011-1014) in 1913 to the Oakland, Antioch & Eastern and also OA&E's parlor-observation-dining car, *Moraga*. The East Shore & Suburban, a Key System predecessor, had three streetcars (Key 426-428) from Brill's Danville Car Company in Danville, Illinois. The existence of cars in California from the Elizabeth, New Jersey, builder, John Stephenson, which Brill acquired in 1904, is uncertain. Sources show that P&SR 51, 53, 55 and 57 were built in 1904 by American Car Company but they are shown in a Stephenson catalog.

Secondhand Rolling Stock

Because of the general economic weakness of the electric railway industry there was a lively secondhand market for rolling stock, although some of the more interesting acquisitions were due to unusual circumstances.

For example, after the 1906 fire, Pat Calhoun, president of the United Railroads of San Francisco, toured midwestern carbuilding plants looking for rolling stock and placing orders for new cars. Fifty streetcars for Chicago City Railway, the first cars in an order for 200, were nearing completion at the American Car Company plant in St. Louis. Because of the emergency in San Francisco, the Chicago traction company, as a gesture of goodwill to stricken San Francisco, allowed Calhoun to purchase the cars, and they became the 1500-1549 in San Francisco.

Calhoun also discovered 12 brand-new interurban cars at the St. Louis Car Company plant. These cars were part of an order placed by the fiscally embarrassed Philadelphia & Western, then building between 69th Street at Upper Darby in Philadelphia and Strafford. Calhoun bought these cars (URR 1-12) for the San Mateo interurban line where customers nicknamed them "Big Subs." Four other cars from the P&W order were bought from St. Louis by the Northern Electric and were NE (later SN) 106-109.

During the mid-1930s URR successor Market Street Railway bought a number of streetcars from Williamsport, Pennsylvania, and East St. Louis, Illinois, because they could be operated without conductors. Most of these cars ran but a few years in San Francisco because of the reimposition of a city ordinance prohibiting one-man operation that was not repealed until 1954.

The Key System had secondhand cars from Lehigh Valley Transit in Pennsylvania, Washington Water Power in Spokane and the Sacramento Northern. During World War II, the U.S. Maritime Commission sent 90 former New York elevated rapid transit cars to Key System, which used them to the Henry J. Kaiser shipyards at Richmond.

The San Francisco Municipal Railway acquired 70 PCC cars secondhand from St. Louis Public Service

between 1957 and 1962, and in 1974 acquired 11 PCCs from Toronto. Those cars were thirdhand as Toronto had bought them in 1957 from Kansas City Public Service.

Southern Pacific often transferred cars among the systems it owned on the West Coast. Pacific Electric received interurban cars from SP's Portland, Oregon, suburban service when it was abandoned in 1929, and some San Jose cars over the years. Most of SP's Oakland suburban cars found their way to Pacific Electric during World War II along with the 19 steel and aluminum Northwestern Pacific cars.

The United Railroads sold many of its small cars to California operators, among them Eureka and Santa Cruz. At least some of the Santa Cruz cars first were sold by URR to Northern Electric which used them in Chico, then sold them to Santa Cruz.

San Diego was less than satisfied with Birney cars and sold some to the Sacramento Northern, Oklahoma City and Southern Pacific; some San Diego interurban cars ended up on Pacific Electric. During World War II, former New York City, Wilkes-Barre and ex-Salt Lake City streetcars were sent to San Diego to handle wartime traffic.

The Visalia Electric sold four interurban cars to the Pacific Electric which resold two of them to the San Francisco & Napa Valley. A railroad in Argentina bought a number of California electric railway cars including 28 PE Hollywood center-door cars, the 50 PE 1100-type interurbans that had run to Pasadena, the 30 PCC cars PE bought for Glendale-Burbank service and two electric locomotives. Thirty-one Key System Bay Bridge cars were acquired by the same Argentina company. PE also sold eight Hollywood cars to the Portland-Oregon City interurban line, which also had a former Key System streetcar for about 10 years. Vera Cruz also bought 15 streetcars from PE.

Accidents

California's electric railways were an extremely safe method of transport. Major accidents occurred infrequently and through the history of electric traction in the state there were only five terrible disasters, a good record considering that the poor earnings of the industry often led to deferred maintenance and obsolete and worn-out rolling stock being used. Much of the credit for safe operation is due to the dedication of employees who, while realizing that their railroads had no hope of survival, still paid close attention to safety.

The worst accident, in loss of life, occurred on the San Francisco & Napa Valley, then the San Francisco, Napa &

Calistoga, on June 19, 1913. Thirteen persons were killed and 28 injured when two trains met head-on two miles north of Vallejo.

A few weeks later, on July 13, 1913, 12 persons were killed and 200 were injured in a rear-end collision of two Pacific Electric trains at Vineyard in western Los Angeles.

Even slow-moving streetcar systems had major tragedies. Five persons were killed and 30 injured on Easter Sunday, April 10, 1904, when an out-of-control Santa Barbara streetcar overturned on a curve. The worst streetcar accident occurred on July 13, 1918, when the air brakes apparently failed on a United Railroads of San Francisco car on the rural Visitacion Valley line. Eight passengers were killed and 70 others were injured when the car overturned on a curve.

The last major electric railway accident in California occurred on December 4, 1924. A San Francisco-Sacramento Railroad (Sacramento Northern) interurban train rammed into the rear of a Key System train stopped on the approach to the Key System ferry pier, killing 10 persons and seriously injuring about 40 others. The signaling system was set for 35-mile-an-hour trains but the interurban was capable of 55 miles an hour and could not stop in time.

After the Napa Valley accident, the road was forced into fiscal reorganization because company officials were blamed for not properly training crew members. In the aftermath of the PE wreck at Vineyard, the company installed automatic signals and bought only all-steel interurban cars, which were far safer. The United Railroads accident was a mystery and there were allegations that German sympathizers sabotaged the car because many of the riders were working in shipyards and industries vital to World War I efforts. The car involved did not have a conductor and the accident was the major reason oneman cars were barred in San Francisco until 1954. After the Key System accident, a speed limit was imposed and the signals were altered to provide more space between trains.

DISINTEGRATION BEGINS

It would be difficult to pinpoint when the disintegration of California's electric railway industry began. Early warning signs were not understood or perhaps in some cases were ignored. Electric railways nationally were hit hard by the inflation that followed World War I, which caused sharp increases in labor and material costs. Industry executives saw these conditions as being temporary and expected the economy to level off.

A clear example of miscalculation was the street railway industry's reaction to the Jitney craze around the time of World War I. Jitneys were the first taste of competition streetcar companies had faced and the unregulated automobiles stole passengers from regulated street railways. The problem soon disappeared because of regulation, but what streetcar executives did not understand was that the Jitney was a sign that the days of transportation monopoly were over.

The shortsighted attitude is clearly evident in interviews conducted by the *Electric Railway Journal* in 1920 for two articles, "California and Her Tractions." Both Paul Shoup, president of the Pacific Electric (and later of the Southern Pacific) and William Von Phul, president of the United Railroads, told writer Edward Hungerford that "the traction systems of California have seen their hardest days." The PE, Los Angeles Railway, United Railroads, Municipal Railway and others reported that revenues were rising after a brief interlude of poor earnings.

The figures, Shoup said,

> mean that the peak of the automobile, publicly or privately owned or operated, has been reached out here—and passed.

About 500,000 automobiles were registered "for pleasure purposes" in California in 1920 and this number "increases by 100,000 during tourist season," the PE executive said. To this, writer Hungerford added:

> I think I can follow Mr. Shoup perfectly. On a glorious California Sunday in May we drove out together from San Francisco in the Santa Clara Valley toward San Jose. The excellent highways were thronged with cars. Yet driving that day was not without its perplexities. Not only was gasoline very high priced—for California—but there was precious little to be obtained at any price. One drove from service station to service station, and occasionally where he was known or favored was grudgingly doled out two or three gallons of the precious fluid. There was not an ounce of it to be spared . . . the gasoline famine was upon the land; a tragedy which traction men, at least, were enabled to regard with complete equanimity.

Hungerford said that street railway and interurban men should not underestimate the threat of the automobile. If gasoline runs short, a "substitute fuel" will be developed, he said. "The highway is bound to be a real competitor of yours for many a year to come."

Neither Hungerford nor probably anyone in the automobile business could foresee what was about to occur. A government-financed road system would be built and soon there would be thousands of service stations and low-cost gasoline. The wave of immigration to Los Angeles during the Great Depression of the 1930s was different from the earlier migrations to California: This time the new citizens came by automobile rather than by rail or ship. They brought their own transportation with them and had no need for electric traction.

The disintegration of passenger service came quickly on even the stronger interurbans. For example, the executives of the San Francisco-Sacramento Railroad, the Oakland-Sacramento predecessor of the Sacramento Northern, were optimistic in their first annual report. The new railroad had just assumed control of the fiscally troubled Oakland, Antioch & Eastern and, at the close of 1920, passenger business was on the rise. The executives observed that

> passenger earnings increased from $852,250.30 in 1919 . . . to $976,752.18 in 1920. An increase of 20 percent in rates was granted to the railroad on August 26, 1920. However, we note that the passenger earnings had increased before these rates took effect and it is believed that these increased passenger earnings are due to the improvements in the roadbed and the increased publicity your railroad is receiving by reason of keeping to schedule time.

The situation was far different only four years later. Passenger revenues had dropped to $759,051.37, and

DOWN THE TREE-LINED median of Euclid Avenue in Ontario comes No. 177, built initially for Southern Pacific's East Bay electric network, in 1912. This local route, which provided connections to PE's San Bernardino line, disappeared in 1924 along with many other local rail services—victims of a drought and changing times.   *Craig Rasmussen Collection*

company officials observed in the 1923 annual report that

> the immediate future of the passenger business is . . . difficult to anticipate owing to the progress of the automobile industry and the good roads in the state. In 1916 there were 10 automobiles to every 100 persons in California. At the present time there are about 33 automobiles to every 100 persons and every owner of an automobile is related, presumably, to two or three persons to whom his automobile is available, thus making an automobile possible to practically every person in the state . . . if the rate of automobiles per capita continues to increase faster than the growth of population, further decline in passenger business might be expected.

The SF-S did not fare well and was in deep financial trouble by 1927 when investors allied with the Western Pacific bought the company. WP had owned the old Northern Electric (reorganized as Sacramento Northern Railroad in 1918) since 1921 and renamed it Sacramento Northern Railway in 1925, when the Interstate Commerce Commission officially approved the acquisition. Had WP not acquired the two interurbans and merged them in 1929 as Sacramento Northern Railway, it is doubtful they would have operated passenger service as long as they did and that abandonment would have come in the early 1930s rather than in 1940 and 1941.

By the mid-1920s, the trend was manifest and it was obvious it could not be reversed by the mid-1930s. For the most part, it was clear that it was just a matter of time before even the strongest companies would lose their passenger markets to the automobile. Eventually, equipment and track would wear out and there would be no money to repair or replace it.

LINES DISAPPEAR

Pacific Electric abandoned its Pomona streetcars in 1924. The often forgotten Glendale & Montrose was abandoned in 1930 and another obscure operation, the rural line between Grass Valley and Nevada City never reopened after a heavy snowstorm in 1923. The Watsonville line died in 1917 and the Pacific Coast electric line quit in 1928. By 1935, the P&SR, Traction Co., Visalia Electric, Tidewater Southern and Peninsular Railway had discontinued interurban passenger service.

Then between 1935 and 1941, the Napa Valley, Northwestern Pacific and SP ended their Bay Area interurban and suburban operations and the Sacramento Northern suspended all interurban service but kept its local street-

cars for a few years. The Pacific Electric invested heavily in buses and abandoned passenger electric service to Whittier, La Habra, Fullerton, from Van Nuys to Canoga Park and Van Nuys to San Fernando. Los Angeles-Redondo Beach, Los Angeles-Alhambra-Temple City and L.A.-San Bernardino service also disappeared. Streetcars now were gone from many cities, including Long Beach, Eureka, Stockton, Fresno and Pasadena.

Marysville-Yuba City and Bakersfield would abandon streetcars in 1942 and Riverside-Corona in 1943, but most cutbacks planned elsewhere were stalled by the impact of World War II.

As soon as the war ended in 1945, the abandonments resumed. Oakland's streetcars were scrapped in 1948 and the Key System trains on the Bay Bridge were discontinued 10 years later. San Francisco merged its Municipal Railway into the Market Street Railway in 1944 and five years later the last Market Street Railway line was converted to bus. San Francisco continued abandonments into the 1950s and only five lines—four of them using tunnels—survived after 1956.

The abandonments in Oakland and Los Angeles were probably hastened by the ownership of Los Angeles Transit Lines (ex-Los Angeles Railway) and Key System by pro-bus National City Lines, which was allied with major bus and tire makers and fuel companies.

The Pacific Electric, which parent SP contended lost money each year since 1916 except for the World War II period and 1923 and 1948, was quickly destroyed after World War II. Between 1946 and 1953, PE abandoned 16 major rail lines, including the busy Pasadena routes. Then in 1953 PE sold its rail and bus passenger operations to Jesse L. Haugh, a former City Lines aide who had converted the San Diego rail system to bus in 1949 and promised the same fate for the remaining PE rail lines. Haugh's Metropolitan Coach Lines abandoned the former PE Hollywood Boulevard-Beverly Hills line in 1954 and junked the Glendale-Burbank routes in 1955. These two abandonments left vacant the old PE Subway Terminal on Hill Street in downtown Los Angeles.

What Haugh was unable to accomplish, a new public agency, the Los Angeles Metropolitan Transit Authority, was able to complete. Between 1958 and 1961, LAMTA axed the last PE rail lines, to Watts, Bellflower, San Pedro and Long Beach. At the LAMTA takeover in 1958, only five narrow-gauged lines from the old LARY system were still running and the public agency replaced them with buses in 1963.

The last small town systems were discontinued in 1947 in Chico and Sacramento. After the LAMTA streetcar abandonments in 1963, the only electric passenger railway in California was the San Francisco Municipal Railway, which ran five streetcar lines with 105 PCC cars.

REBIRTH BEGINS WITH BART

But the year before the LAMTA action, there was an election in the three central counties on San Francisco Bay. The electorate approved a $792 million bond issue to be repaid with property taxes. When the bond money was combined with revenue bonds and toll bridge revenues, nearly $1 billion was to be available to build a 75-mile rail rapid transit network. This was to be the system called BART, for Bay Area Rapid Transit and, while it has not lived up to all its promises, BART represents a major rebirth of electric traction in the United States.

Ultimately BART spent $1.6 billion to build what it promised voters in 1962, a 71.5-mile rail rapid transit system and 3.5 miles of subway for San Francisco streetcars. The new rail system, which opened in stages between 1972 and 1974, was plagued by technical problems perhaps because it ignored old and proven technological standards. Besides selecting a complicated "hands-off" control system that gave motormen little to do in the fully automatic operation, third-rail powered BART adopted a wide gauge (5'6") and nonstandard 1,000 volts DC.

The 600-volt Muni subway opened between 1980 and 1982, however, it had standard track gauge and a standard cab-signal system similar to what the Key System used on the Bay Bridge from 1939-1958. Lights inside the cabs of both Key and Muni cars were designed to indicate the safe speed and stop cars automatically if the speed was exceeded. For the subway, Muni acquired 130 articulated cars from Boeing Vertol in Philadelphia that were suitable for both tunnel and on-surface operation.

Because BART and Muni stimulated interest in reviving rail transit, new systems have appeared elsewhere in California. In 1981, a new light rail line opened between San Diego and the Mexican border. In 1986, the San Diego system opened an extension, new 750-volt DC light rail lines were being built in San Jose and Sacramento, and groundbreaking had occurred for a Los Angeles-Long Beach line. There still was serious talk of building a subway under Wilshire Boulevard to the San Fernando Valley in Los Angeles. The scale was far smaller than in the great days early in the 20th century, but electric traction was still functioning in the Golden State and approaching its centennial.

BART BROUGHT California the fast-paced environment of big city rapid transit, with thousands of commuters streaming through fare collection machines in vast underground stations. This scene is at Montgomery Street station under Market Street in downtown San Francisco in 1975.
Harre W. Demoro

North Coast Traction

THE NORTHERNMOST electric railway in California was the Eureka streetcar system, which opened officially on September 15, 1903, and was abandoned on February 20, 1940. When the railway began as Humboldt Transit Company, Eureka was one of the most remote cities in the West. The city's primary connection to the outside world came from the lumber schooners and other coastwise vessels that docked on Humboldt Bay. This changed dramatically in 1914 when the Northwestern Pacific Railroad completed its 285-mile railroad from San Francisco. The earthquake of April 18, 1906, which caused great havoc in the San Francisco Bay Area, was strong enough to knock a statue awry atop the Humboldt County Court House. Two Eureka streetcars acquired from the San Francisco & San Mateo Electric Railway were posed, opposite, in front of the damaged building on that fateful day. One of the cars bought new for the line from Holman Car Company between 1904 and 1910, below, awaited passengers on E Street in 1938.

Below, Waldemar Sievers; opposite, Ted Wurm Collection

HUMBOLDT TRANSIT sold out to the city for $111,539 in 1921 and the system slowly deteriorated in the damp coastal fog. A car rolled on a dirt street, opposite, top, past typical wooden houses in 1938. The weary look of the 19, above, was typical in the final years. An attempt to burn car 18, right, on February 24, 1940, to mark the end of rail service, almost ended in tragedy when the fire began scorching downtown buildings. Work car 01 was used to repair overhead wire and was rebuilt from a San Francisco & San Mateo car.

Opposite, below, Doug Richter;
others, Waldemar Sievers

"Out Market!"
Was The Call
At The Ferry

THE FERRY LOOP at the foot of Market Street was San Francisco's busiest streetcar terminal, with gray-colored Municipal Railway cars (left) and the "White Front" cars of the Market Street Railway screeching around the curves at split-second intervals. The ground collectors, men who urged people toward the cars and collected their fares at the same time, had voices as rough as gravel and as loud as a foghorn. They shouted endlessly: "This car, this car! Out Market! All the way out Market!" Millions of commuters streamed off the ferries from Oakland, Alameda and Sausalito each year, making the Ferry Building one of the busiest passenger terminals in the world. As late as 1936, when this picture was taken, the Ferry Building was still a busy place, but Oakland and Alameda commuter ferries were discontinued in 1939 and the Sausalito boats stopped in 1941. Many of the streetcar lines were rerouted to the new Bay Bridge electric train terminal at First and Mission streets, where the loaders still barked "Out Market!" On the page opposite, the congestion that gave Market Street a "big city" atmosphere in the 1930s is evident. Pedestrians stream across Third Street while three "White Front" Market Street Railway cars roll along Market Street and two gray Municipal Railway streetcars pass in the background on Geary Street. There were four tracks on Market Street; the Municipal system ran on the outside tracks and the private company used the inside pair. *Above, Ralph W. Demoro; opposite, Charles A. Smallwood Collection*

The United Went Almost Everywhere

SAN FRANCISCO'S largest streetcar system was the United Railroads, which was reorganized in 1921 as the Market Street Railway and acquired by the city and merged into the Municipal Railway in 1944. It was inevitable that the Municipal Railway would prevail: a city charter provision called for municipal ownership of all utilities, and changing economics eventually made public transit unprofitable and in need of a steady government subsidy. The combined systems carried a record 227.4 million passengers in 1945. However, when these photographs were taken early in the 20th century, the threat of a city-owned streetcar system seemed remote. On this page, one of the 200 cars bought by the URR in 1906-07 – in the largest streetcar order in the history of the West – pauses on Market Street at 4th and Eddy streets in 1908, a decade before the upstart Municipal Railway would add two tracks to the city's main thoroughfare and create a four-track streetcar street. The Humboldt Bank Building tower rises above the westbound car. On the opposite page, the 136, fresh and glossy from the Jewett factory in Newark, Ohio, approaches the sharp curve at Presidio Avenue and Jackson Street on June 7, 1911. In the photo below, the URR sightseeing car *Golden Gate* pauses at Land's End so riders can see the great Pacific Ocean and inhale the salt air in 1908.

Three photos, Charles A. Smallwood Collection

MOST OF SAN FRANCISCO'S street railway was cable-operated before the 1906 fire. Reconstruction following the disaster involved building an almost entirely new electric system. The United Railroads carefully recorded the progress for investors back east with glass plate negatives, from which these three prints were made. On this page, the first electric car on Gough Street is surrounded by company officials and local merchants on December 22, 1910. San Bruno Avenue at Courtland Avenue, opposite, had a rural look in 1912 when the URR photographer recorded a turnout switch that allowed cars to pass on the single-tracked 25 line. Posters for William Howard Taft's unsuccessful attempt to win reelection to the presidency are on the fence at left. In the bottom frame, a southbound streetcar on Montgomery Street approaches Clay Street on July 25, 1914. The Montgomery Block, the four-story building to the right of the streetcar, was built early in the city's history and survived the 1906 fire. *Three photos, Charles A. Smallwood Collection*

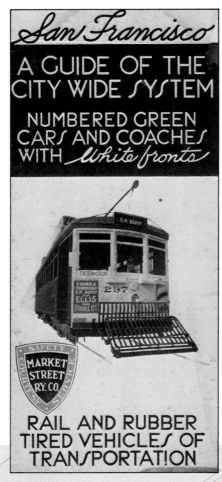

San Francisco
A GUIDE OF THE CITY WIDE SYSTEM
NUMBERED GREEN CARS AND COACHES WITH *White fronts*

SAFETY
MARKET STREET RY. CO.
COURTESY SERVICE

RAIL AND RUBBER TIRED VEHICLES OF TRANSPORTATION

MARKET STREET RAILWAY cars had a distinctive "White Front" and green paint scheme that was even promoted on the covers of system maps in the mid-1930s. The variety of Market Street Railway operations in that period is depicted on these two pages. Below, a 22-Fillmore streetcar exchanges passengers at Broadway and Fillmore Street with a tiny counterbalance electric car that will creep down steep Fillmore Hill tethered to a safety cable under the street. When the car begins its descent from Broadway, a second car will start its uphill climb from the bottom of the grade, two blocks away at Green Street. Both cars were attached to the same cable to "counterbalance" each other. On the opposite page, the conductor raises the trolley pole on one of the high-platform 700-type cars that were constructed in 1918-19 on the frames of electric cars built in 1894 for Mission Street. Car 757 is at Waller and Stanyan streets; above is the new double wire for the city's first trolley bus line, which began operating on October 6, 1935. Because of steep grades, the 33 rail line had to see-saw back and forth on a switchback at Market and Clayton streets to gain elevation for its journey over Twin Peaks. The little car in the bottom photo is on the Divisadero Street extension, a three-block line between Jackson and Sacramento streets that was abandoned in the early 1930s. *Map, Harre W. Demoro Collection; photos, this page, Waldemar Sievers; page opposite, Ralph W. Demoro*

A "COMFORT CAR" built in the company shops in 1923 clatters past an old brick warehouse on Sansome Street in 1939. The building dates from the sailing ship era when grain-carrying and other sailing ships docked nearby on The Embarcadero. Right, a Daly City-bound car also built by the company approaches the Southern Pacific overpass on 30th Street after crossing Dolores Street. San Francisco's only interurban service was the 40 line, which opened in 1903 to San Mateo. It usually had 1200-type cars acquired in 1903 from the Laclede Car Company in St. Louis, Missouri. Car 1237 loaded at the downtown terminal on Fifth Street at Market Street in 1938 in the top view, opposite page. In the frame below, taken in 1947 after the Municipal Railway had acquired the Market Street Railway and repainted the 1225 blue and cream, a San Francisco-bound schedule loaded at one of the 40 line's major traffic generators, the Roman Catholic Holy Cross Cemetery at Colma, south of Daly City.

Four photos, Waldemar Sievers

THE TWO CARS on the opposite page came to San Francisco almost immediately after the earthquake and fire of 1906. Crew members are posing with a "Big Sub," one of 12 cars built in 1906 by the St. Louis Car Company for the Philadelphia & Western Railway. The photo below shows Market Street Railway 1517, one of 50 cars from an order that Chicago City Railways had placed with American Car Company. The cars had been diverted to San Francisco as a gesture of goodwill during the emergency. On this page, one of the last cars built by the Market Street Railway's Elkton Shops is displayed at Haight and Stanyan streets in 1933. The home-built cars used mechanical and electrical components salvaged from obsolete rolling stock. The all-white car below is the *San Francisco*, which was built in 1901 by the St. Louis Car Company and rebuilt by the United Railroads in 1904. In the 1920s the car was "given" to the city's schoolchildren, who rode it for free on outings and field trips.

Page opposite, top, Charles A. Smallwood Collection; below, Ralph W. Demoro; this page, top, Ralph W. Demoro; bottom, Waldemar Sievers

"Sunny Jim" Paid First Muni Fare

HIS HONOR, Mayor James (Sunny Jim) Rolph, Jr., was determined to build a "people's railway," a streetcar system owned by its riders. He is credited with dropping the first nickel into the farebox on the very first Municipal Railway car which departed from Kearny, Geary and Market streets on December 28, 1912. One of the big Muni cars built in 1923 at the Bethlehem Shipyard, painted blue and gold, took the Ferry Building curve in 1946. Like most San Francisco cars in the heyday of electric traction, this one is big and heavy (almost 26 tons), and, while it has its loading and unloading platforms near street level, its riders must climb an inside step to reach the passenger area. On the page opposite, one of Muni's original cars built in 1911 by Holman, another hometown builder, exits the Stockton Street Tunnel at Sutter Street en route to Market Street in 1935. The car carries Muni's original gray paint scheme, which led patrons to refer to the city-owned streetcars as "Battleships." Directly above the car and behind the Navarre Hotel to the left is a short alley named Burritt Street, where Brigid O'Shaughnessy murdered Sam Spade's partner, Miles Archer, in Dashiell Hammett's classic novel, *The Maltese Falcon*. The little two-axle, center-door car was one of 21 cars acquired in 1921 and 1922 for the hilly E-Union Street line.

Above, Ralph W. Demoro; opposite, Waldemar Sievers

ON THE DAY the Treasure Island fair opened—February 18, 1939—some Municipal Railway cars at the Scott and Chestnut streets terminal of the F-Stockton line were carrying dash signs advising they ran to the exposition ferries at the Ferry Building. The F-Stockton line's usual downtown destination was at Stockton and Market streets. The first car is Muni No. 1, built in 1912 by Holman and preserved in 1985 by the City and County of San Francisco. The F's downtown terminal is shown in the top view, opposite page. The camera looks north, straight up Stockton Street. The Muni car on the right is headed out Market Street on the L-Taraval line to the zoo in 1945. In the last days of the four tracks on Market Street, the variety of paint schemes is evident at Fifth and Market streets, where the columns of the J.C. Penney store dominate the intersection. The car on the left is of Muni origin and is decked out in the postwar green and cream scheme, while the ex-Market Street Railway car in the center has a blue and yellow front and green sides. The car on the right, also of Muni origin, is in the blue and gold colors adopted in the late 1930s. The photo was taken in 1948.

Both pages, Waldemar Sievers

THE LONG GEARY STREET lines that evolved out of Muni's first route of 1912 survived until 1956 and were abandoned mainly because the city wanted to reconstruct portions of the street and because the proposed Bay Area Rapid Transit (BART) line to Marin County was supposed to use the thoroughfare. Shortly before the line was abandoned, inbound 111 paused at Geary Boulevard and Baker Street. The car was one of 125 cars Muni acquired from Ohio-based builder Jewett in 1914 for a major expansion program that included service to the 1915 Panama-Pacific International Exposition and the new J-Church and Twin Peaks Tunnel lines. On the opposite page, the same car awaited riders at the Playland-at-the-Beach terminal on a foggy morning in 1954. Generations of San Franciscans remember Playland's death-defying roller coaster. In the bottom view, two cars also built by Jewett in 1914 pass on 33rd Avenue at Balboa Street in 1954.

Above, John N. Harder; opposite, Harre W. Demoro

TWIN PEAKS TUNNEL was Muni's major public works project until the Market Street subway was built in the 1960s and 1970s. The tunnel, almost two miles long and with stations at Eureka Street and Forest Hill, was completed in 1917 and opened in 1918. Both portals were demolished as part of the Market Street subway work. On the page opposite, Muni 1146, a former St. Louis Public Service car of PCC design, emerges from the Castro Street portal in 1970. On this page, an L-Taraval car unloads at West Portal at Ulloa Street and West Portal Avenue in 1947. In the view below, a PCC Car built new in 1951 for the Muni swings onto Ulloa Street on the L-Taraval line en route to the ocean beach and zoo in 1968.

Opposite and below, this page, Harre W. Demoro;
above, Waldemar Sievers

"LIGHT RAIL," a new word for San Francisco traction, was introduced to the Bay City in 1978-79 with the arrival of the first of 130 six-axle, articulated cars constructed by Boeing Vertol. The cars were designed both for high-platform subway operation and street running and had center steps that could be adjusted for subway and street running. The cars accelerated slower than the PCC cars they replaced, but their top speed of 50 miles an hour made them good performers in the subway and in Twin Peaks and Sunset Tunnels. Municipal Railway officials, mindful of the technical bugs that had marred BART, introduced the cars at a leisurely pace, and it was not until February 18, 1981, that the N-Judah line was converted to subway-surface operation with the new equipment. Opening day at Embarcadero station, one of four Market Street stops shared with BART (Muni is on the upper level, BART is below), is shown on this page. On the opposite page, two cars meet on the M line private right-of-way at St. Francis Circle (Junipero Serra Boulevard and Sloat Boulevard) during tests on March 5, 1980. In the bottom photo, a K line car pauses at West Portal station, built in the hillside after the portal on page 49 was demolished. The 1200-series cars were built originally for Muni but the 1300 series were intended for Boston's MBTA system and sold instead to San Francisco.

Both pages, Harre W. Demoro

The Empire Built With Borax Wealth

ACROSS SAN FRANCISCO BAY from the big city were the growing suburbs of the East Bay, where Francis Marion (Borax) Smith, who became a millionaire after discovering borax deposits in Nevada and eastern California, was quick to take advantage of real estate opportunities. Smith amalgamated local streetcar lines in the 1890s, then built the San Francisco, Oakland & San Jose Railway—the "Key Route"—from 1903 to 1911, and went broke soon thereafter. The 10-car train of orange wooden Key Route cars on this page is loaded with University of California cadets returning to the Berkeley campus from the Panama-Pacific International Exposition in San Francisco in 1915. On the page opposite, one of the 88 streamlined units built in the 1930s for operation on the Bay Bridge crosses Howe Street and enters the deep cut in the hillside that brings the train to Broadway in 1953. In the bottom view, two of the Key's highly successful center-door 650-style cars roll into the 40th and San Pablo station in 1935 en route to the ferry pier. Almost 99 million passengers were carried on the streetcars in 1925. In 1924, the peak year for the train-ferry service, 18.1 transbay riders were recorded. The all-time transbay rail record was set in 1945 when almost 26.5 million rode Bay Bridge trains. *Above, Vernon J. Sappers Collection; opposite, top, Harre W. Demoro; below, Ralph W. Demoro*

THE HISTORY OF THE Piedmont Extension is recorded in the two photos on this page. On November 2, 1924, Key System and civic officials gathered around the first train to go over the new line from 41st Street and Piedmont Avenue through the Piedmont residential area to Oakland Avenue. In the view at left, the last train approached the same Oakland Avenue location on April 19, 1958. Buses took over as soon as this final train departed for San Francisco. One of Borax Smith's dreams was to build an interurban line south for 50 miles to San Jose. The signal bridge on the page opposite was built to control the junction at 40th Street with a line that was never constructed. The bridge is shown about 1910 when the area still was mostly open country, and in 1955 when the tracks were in the midst of Emeryville's industrial area. The steel bridge was removed after Key abandoned rail service in 1958. The right-of-way shown in the photos at Oakland Avenue also was to be part of the never-built San Jose line.   *Left, Howard Erker, Oakland Tribune;*
above, W. E. Gardiner;
opposite, top, Vernon J. Sappers Collection;
below, Harre W. Demoro

THE PIER TERMINAL, at the end of a causeway and trestle nearly three miles from the Oakland-Emeryville shoreline, was the hub of Key System's transbay operation until Bay Bridge rails were finished in 1939. On this page, passengers getting off the ferry from San Francisco scurry toward waiting electric trains—a transfer that took only a minute or two in 1913. On the page opposite are views of the pier and approach trestle in the late 1930s, after a new trainshed had replaced the one destroyed by a fire in 1933. A train of new streamlined cars acquired for service on the new San Francisco-Oakland Bay Bridge, shown behind the trestle, approaches the causeway in 1937. A year earlier, the bridge casts an ominous shadow over the ferry pier seen from the deck of a departing steamer. The bridge was opened to vehicular traffic in 1936 but not to electric trains until 1939.   *Above, Vernon J. Sappers Collection;*
opposite, Ralph W. Demoro

WOODEN INTERURBAN CARS with arched windows and decorative interior woodwork were acquired in several orders for Key Route service between 1903 and 1912. With their high end steps, the cars were more suited to intercity service, such as the proposed San Jose extension, than the high-density suburban service that was to be their fate. Passengers rode on rattan upholstered seats in the early days, as shown at right. This car was built in the company shops, but it followed blueprints for earlier cars built by the St. Louis Car Company. The cars had flickering arc lights suspended in globes from the ceiling for illumination. Even near the end of their long careers, the 500-class cars were well maintained and retained their balanced appearance. The 577, above, is crossing Adeline Street in Emeryville in 1936. On the page opposite are Key's later transbay cars, constructed in 1917, 1923 and 1925. The center-door cars could be coupled with the older 500-type cars, as in the train above on Poplar Street in Oakland about 1925. The cars were supposed to look like streetcars, to quiet objections from Oakland officials over long trains running in the 12th Street business district. Framing from 10 of these cars was used to construct five of the new Bay Bridge trains in 1937. The 678, bottom, shows the cars in their final months, with air-operated slider pantograph and a special coupler that automatically made air and electrical connections between cars.

Above, Ralph W. Demoro;
bottom, Gordon Robertson Collection;
opposite, top, Charles A. Smallwood Collection;
bottom, L. L. Bonney

THE BAY BRIDGE had a profound impact on the Key System's transbay rail lines. On January 15, 1939, commuter ferry service was discontinued and all service to San Francisco was switched onto tracks the Key shared on the lower deck of the bridge with the Southern Pacific (Interurban Electric Railway) and Sacramento Northern. Starting in December 1936, Key acquired 88 two-compartment, articulated units for bridge service. Units numbered 100-124 had straight sides, but 125-187 were more streamlined with slanted sides and wider windows. All but 165-187 were equipped with mechanical and electrical components salvaged from retired 500 and 650-type cars, and 100-104 used frames and side sections from ten 650-type cars. To the passenger, the cars all looked the same,

and interiors, below, were bright and comfortable, with cane seats in the smoking section and leather seats in the non-smoker. Both views on this page were taken at Wilmington, Delaware, just before the first unit was shipped from the Bethlehem Steel Harlan plant. San Francisco had a low skyline in 1939, page opposite, as a train from downtown Oakland rolls over the viaduct toward the First and Mission Streets elevated terminal. Key is using 600-volt third rail; the overhead catenary is for the IER and SN 1200-volt trains. A Trestle Glen-bound train heads toward Oakland on the lower deck of the Bay Bridge in 1954.   *This page, Harre W. Demoro Collection; opposite, top, Waldemar Sievers; bottom, Harre W. Demoro*

THE KEY SYSTEM WAS built before there were very many automobiles, and much of its trackage was in city streets, where traffic congestion slowed schedules and resulted in delays—a situation that hastened the April 20, 1958, abandonment of the service. San Francisco-bound 165 is in the middle of Shattuck Avenue in Berkeley, in 1954. The rails were built for the Southern Pacific in 1911, and turned over to Key System when the Interurban Electric Railway quit in 1941. Berkeley's Adeline Street had six tracks, two for Key trains, two for Key streetcars and a pair for the SP. On the left is one of Key's steeple-cab electric motors used to switch industrial sidings and the quarries at Leona Heights in the hills behind Mills College. The unusual looking train of ex-New York elevated cars, opposite top, is from the Shipyard Railway, which the Key operated from 1943-45 to the Kaiser Shipyards in Richmond. Below, a lightweight 900-type streetcar equipped with a pantograph awaited passengers in 1941 on the little-used G-Westbrae shuttle between Albany and Berkeley.

Above, Harre W. Demoro; below, Vernon J. Sappers;
opposite, top, Ralph W. Demoro; bottom, Ted Wurm

STREETCARS DOMINATED downtown Oakland in the mid-1920s, as at the busy junction of 14th Street and Broadway. Although the streetcars and transbay rail operation were owned by the same company, they often were run as independent enterprises, sometimes even with different names and paint schemes. The streetcar in its infancy is illustrated on the opposite page, top, with a "California Type" car of the Oakland Street Railroad on Park Boulevard—then Fourth Avenue—in the 1890s. Oakland High School later occupied the knoll behind the two-axle car, which carries a window poster advertising People's Theater, where *Queena* was to perform. Below is an open breezer of the Oakland, San Leandro & Hayward's Electric Railway—the longest electric railway in the world at its opening in 1892. These open cars were more popular on the hot and humid East Coast than in California, where the climate was milder.   *Above, Harre W. Demoro Collection; opposite, Vernon J. Sappers Collection*

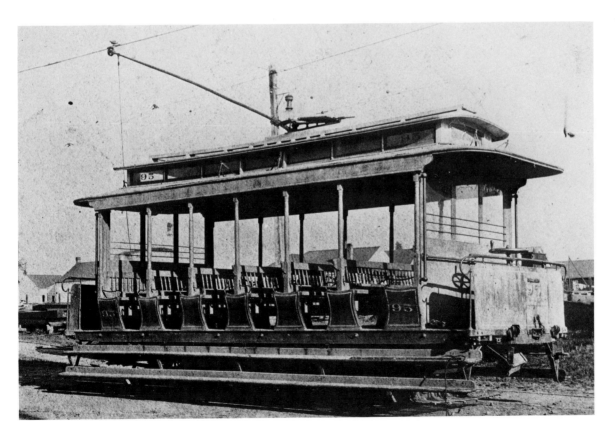

WASHINGTON STREET is crowded with shoppers as a new PAYE (Pay-As-You Enter) streetcar creeps toward 14th Street. These 60 streetcars, built by St. Louis Car Company in 1911, were among the first on the West Coast to have the conductor stand on the rear platform and watch boarding passengers deposit their fares in a box. Previously, the conductor walked through the car to lift fares. Oakland converted its streetcars to one-man operation about 1930, which is why riders are boarding at the front door of the 928, a lightweight (22 tons) car built in 1923 by American Car Company. The car is headed downtown on Piedmont Avenue at 41st Street, where patrons could transfer from the C-Piedmont transbay train to the local service. *Above, Harre W. Demoro Collection; below, Waldemar Sievers*

WOMEN TOOK OVER many transit jobs during World War II. The Key System assigned them to operate streetcars and buses and to collect fares on transbay trains and at Shipyard Railway stations. One of the newly trained "motormen" posed at the controls of a 1911-vintage 350-class car in Oakland, showing off the uniform with its dressy cap designed especially for female personnel. Just as most people expected they would, most of the women quit the company at war's end, but a few were still driving Oakland buses in the 1970s. A major traffic generator for Oakland's streetcars was the University of California, whose distinctive clock tower is at right. Car 994, built in 1926 by American Car Company, is on the 6-College Avenue line. By the time the photo was taken in 1946, 15 new electric trolley buses had arrived to replace streetcars on the 6 line, but they were never used and sent instead to Los Angeles. Gasoline and diesel buses replaced the streetcars.

Left, Harre W. Demoro Collection; above, Waldemar Sievers

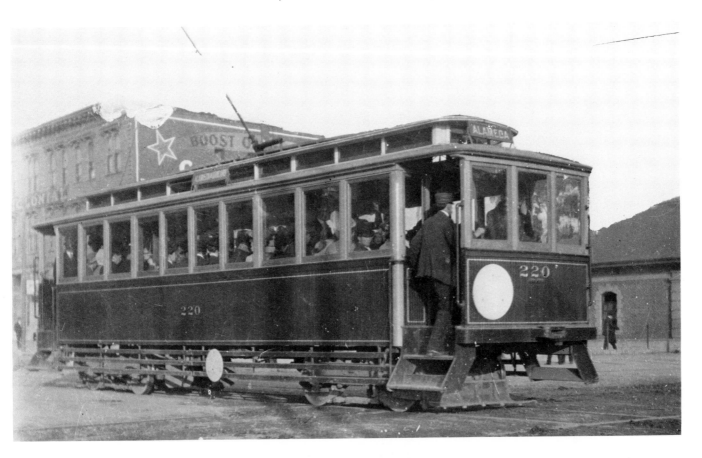

EXCEPT FOR AN experimental car operated briefly during the 1930s, the most modern Oakland streetcars were the 900 series built by American Car Company in 1923 and 1926. Although these cars could be coupled into two-car trains for heavy service, they operated singly and with a one-man crew during most of their careers. They boasted rattan, or cane, seats, opposite, top, and natural wood interior trim. Unlike most Oakland cars—and many elsewhere in California—Key's 95 900-type cars had level floors close to the street and no interior steps. This speeded loading and dramatically reduced boarding and loading accidents. Shortly before all streetcar service ceased in Oakland in 1948, the 960, opposite, below, awaited riders at the Southern Pacific 16th Street station. Two of the dozens of cars built in the company shops are shown on this page. The 220 was rebuilt about 1910 from an old car that had open sections. The design was unpopular because of the high steps, but some of these cars were operated into the mid-1920s. The unusual car built in 1906, with the open center section, was called a "Kelly Car" in honor of its inventor, master mechanic William Kelly. It ran in Alameda-Oakland service for most of its career. *Opposite, top, Harre W. Demoro Collection; below, Waldemar Sievers; above, R. T. Hill; below, Gordon Robertson Collection*

Harriman's Answer Was Red

THE FIRST TIME railroad mogul E. H. Harriman arrived at the Southern Pacific Mole he was pleased at what he saw: here was a monopoly, where huge SP ferries met mainline and suburban trains. Several years later, as the story has it, Harriman again stepped off his elegant car at Oakland Mole, and was astonished to see a long trestle on San Francisco Bay carrying Key Route electric trains to ferries that were faster than the SP boats. He took one look at the grimy steam-operated SP suburban trains and ordered his engineers to modernize the system at once. The result was a magnificent electrified suburban train system that drew its operating techniques and engineering from the best examples on the East Coast, including the electrified lines into New York's Grand Central Terminal and Pennsylvania Station. SP's first electric lines opened in Alameda in 1911; by 1915 the system was complete and considered a marvel of engineering and utility. The first cars were green but they were quickly repainted red for better visibility; the system became known as the "Red Trains" by the public. The first cars had square end windows, but most were fitted with the owl-eyed windows as shown on the opposite page. A typical Seventh Street train, consisting of a combination passenger-baggage motor car, an unpowered trailer, and an all-passenger motor car, speeds toward Oakland Mole (also called Oakland Pier) in 1935. The cars still have knuckle couplers, air brake hoses, sockets for electric cables and low wire gates, which were removed for Bay Bridge service. *Two photos, Ralph W. Demoro*

THE OWL EYES that were a trademark for SP's East Bay "Red Trains" were not a feature of most of the cars when they were new. The two-car train, above, on Webster Street in downtown Oakland in 1911, is still painted green and has roof headlights and roller pantographs. Almost 30 years later, the same style car has been rebuilt with porthole windows, a Westinghouse Air Brake coupler and square destination sign. The last two improvements were made for operation over the San Francisco-Oakland Bay Bridge, which started on January 15, 1939. On the page opposite are two views of the "Red Trains" during the Bay Bridge era. Above, a Berkeley-Ninth Street train exits the Oakland end of the span, and, below, an Alameda-North Side train rolls along Lincoln Avenue toward West Alameda, past an ornate station dating from the steam suburban train days. The SP renamed the system Interurban Electric Railway for bridge operation.   *Above, Harre W. Demoro Collection; below, Ralph W. Demoro; opposite, Waldemar Sievers*

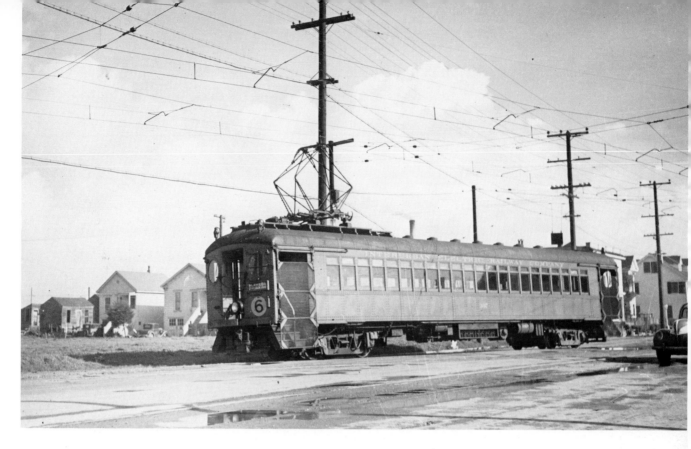

ONE CAR WAS enough most of the time on IER's lightly patronized Alameda lines. Car 307 on the North Side-Lincoln Avenue line is swinging through the vacant lots at the western end of Pacific Avenue in Alameda in 1939, and soon will end its journey that began in downtown San Francisco and included a run over the San Francisco-Oakland Bay Bridge. A three-car

Seventh Street train is exiting the two-level bridge, below, at the Oakland shoreline. IER and Sacramento Northern trains used overhead 1,200-volt catenary on the bridge and Key System trains drew current from a 600-volt third rail. IER and SN quit the bridge railway in 1941 but Key trains ran until 1958.

Above, Robert Searle; below, Waldemar Sievers

FADED RED PAINT on a Dutton Avenue-bound Seventh Street train at Seventh Street and Broadway in Oakland attested to the hard times of the early 1930s. The arched facade on the right locates the SP station, which dated from the steam local era. Car 319, right, was one of the original cars ordered by SP for the electrification. The car was built in 1911 by American Car & Foundry Company. It had Baldwin trucks and General Electric equipment. Aside from the round windows and slider-pantograph, the car, at Alameda Pier in 1937, had changed little from the day it arrived from the builder. The 52-ton car was among those sent to Los Angeles during World War II where it became Pacific Electric 4604, then 417, and finally Los Angeles MTA 1527. The car was finally scrapped in 1959.

Above, Ralph W. Demoro;
right, Waldemar Sievers

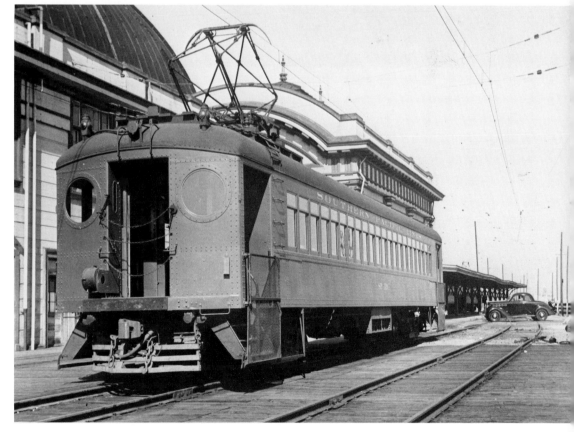

Riding The Longest Interurban

THE MAIN LINE of the Sacramento Northern Railway stretched for 185 miles from San Francisco through the great Sacramento Valley to Chico, and offered the longest interurban ride in the United States. The journey took a little more than six hours. Because the SN was the result of a merger of two major companies, it had two different styles of equipment and even the voltage and method of collecting electricity differed. The train on this page consisted of equipment from both eras: the first, fourth and fifth cars were acquired by the Oakland, Antioch & Eastern for its Oakland-Sacramento 1,200-volt line, which opened in 1913; the second and third were more ornate and were built for the Northern Electric Railway, which opened its Chico-Sacramento line in 1907. Train 27, a local from Concord operated primarily for students at St. Mary's College, rounds the Valle Vista curve above Moraga in 1940. On the page opposite, one of the arch-windowed cars built for the Northern Electric by Niles in 1906 pauses in the arched entrance of the Woodland station on May 26, 1940. The little Birney car passing a "Flying A" gasoline station in Sacramento in 1939 is a typical scene of SN's local streetcar service.

Above, Arthur Alter, courtesy Bay Area Electric R.R. Association; opposite, top, Ted Wurm; bottom, Waldemar Sievers

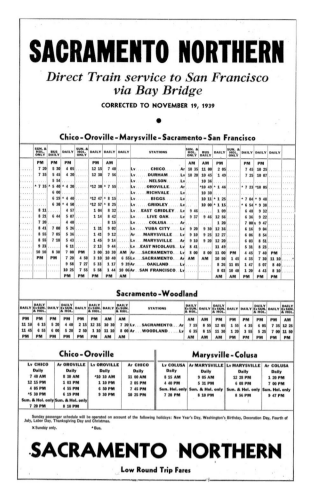

SACRAMENTO NORTHERN

*Direct Train service to San Francisco
via Bay Bridge*

CORRECTED TO NOVEMBER 19, 1939

●

Chico - Oroville - Marysville - Sacramento - San Francisco

SUN. & HOL. ONLY	DAILY	BUS DAILY	DAILY	SUN. & HOL. ONLY	DAILY	DAILY	DAILY		STATIONS			SUN. & HOL. ONLY	BUS DAILY	DAILY	SUN. & HOL. ONLY	DAILY	DAILY	DAILY
PM	PM	PM		PM	AM			Lv	CHICO	Ar	AM	AM	PM		PM	PM		
7 20	5 30	4 05		12 15	7 40			Lv	CHICO	Ar	10 35	11 00	2 05		7 45	10 25		
7 35	5 45	4 20		12 30	7 56			Lv	DURHAM	Lv	10 20	10 45	1 49		7 25	10 07		
	5 54							Lv	NELSON	Lv		10 36						
*7 35	*5 40	*4 20		*12 30	*7 55			Lv	OROVILLE	Ar	*10 49	*1 46		*7 23	*10 05			
	6 00							Lv	RICHVALE	Lv		10 30						
	6 19	*4 40		*12 47	*8 15			Lv	BIGGS	Lv		10 11	*1 25		*7 04	*9 48		
	6 30	*4 50		*12 57	*8 25			Lv	GRIDLEY	Lv		10 00	*1 15		*6 54	*9 38		
8 11		4 57		1 04	8 32			Lv	EAST GRIDLEY	Lv	9 46		1 09		6 48	9 32		
8 21	6 44	5 07		1 14	8 42			Lv	LIVE OAK	Lv	9 37	9 46	12 56		6 36	9 22		
7 20		4 40			8 15			Ar	COLUSA	Ar			1 20		7 00	*9 47		
8 41	7 00	5 26		1 31	9 02			Lv	YUBA CITY	Lv	9 20	9 30	12 36		6 16	9 04		
8 55	7 05	5 36		1 41	9 12			Ar	MARYSVILLE	Lv	9 10	9 25	12 27		6 06	8 54		
8 55	7 10	5 43		1 45	9 14			Ar	MARYSVILLE	Ar	9 10	9 20	12 20		6 03	8 51		
9 23		6 11		2 13	9 44			Lv	EAST NICOLAUS	Lv	8 41		11 49		5 31	8 23		
10 10	8 30	7 00	PM	3 00	10 30	AM		Ar	SACRAMENTO	Lv	8 00	8 00	11 00	PM	4 45	7 40	PM	
PM	PM	7 20	4 50	3 10	10 40	6 55	Lv	SACRAMENTO	Ar	AM	AM	10 50	1 45	4 35	7 30	11 10		
		9 58	7 27	5 33	1 17	9 39	Ar	OAKLAND	Lv			8 26	11 05	1 47	5 07	8 40		
		10 25	7 55	5 58	1 44	10 06	Ar	SAN FRANCISCO	Lv			8 03	10 40	1 20	4 43	8 10		
		PM	PM	PM	AM	AM							AM	AM	PM	PM	PM	

Sacramento - Woodland

DAILY	DAILY Ex SUN. & HOL.	DAILY	DAILY Ex SUN. & HOL.	DAILY	DAILY Ex SUN. & HOL.	DAILY	DAILY Ex SUN. & HOL.		STATIONS		DAILY Ex SUN. & HOL.	DAILY	DAILY Ex SUN. & HOL.	DAILY	DAILY	DAILY	DAILY	DAILY
PM	PM	PM	PM	PM	AM	AM	AM	Lv	SACRAMENTO	Ar	AM	AM	AM	PM	PM	PM	PM	PM
11 10	6 15	5 20	4 40	2 15	12 35	10 30	7 20	Lv	SACRAMENTO	Ar	7 15	8 55	12 05	1 55	4 35	6 05	7 35	12 25
11 45	6 55	6 00	5 20	2 50	1 10	11 10	8 00	Ar	WOODLAND	Lv	6 35	8 15	11 30	1 20	3 55	5 25	7 00	11 50
PM	PM	PM	PM	PM	AM	AM	AM				AM	AM	AM	PM	PM	PM	PM	PM

Chico - Oroville

Lv CHICO Daily	Ar OROVILLE Daily	Lv OROVILLE Daily	Ar CHICO Daily
7 40 AM	8 30 AM	*10 10 AM	11 00 AM
12 15 PM	1 03 PM	1 10 PM	2 05 PM
4 05 PM	4 55 PM	6 50 PM	7 45 PM
*5 30 PM	6 19 PM	9 30 PM	10 25 PM
Sun. & Hol. only 7 20 PM	Sun. & Hol. only 8 10 PM		

Marysville - Colusa

Lv COLUSA Daily	Ar MARYSVILLE Daily	Lv MARYSVILLE Daily	Ar COLUSA Daily
8 15 AM	9 05 AM	12 28 PM	1 20 PM
4 40 PM	5 31 PM	6 08 PM	7 00 PM
Sun. Hol. only 7 20 PM	Sun. & Hol. only 8 10 PM	Sun. & Hol. only 8 56 PM	Sun. Hol. only 9 47 PM

Sunday passenger schedule will be operated on account of the following holidays: New Year's Day, Washington's Birthday, Decoration Day, Fourth of July, Labor Day, Thanksgiving Day and Christmas.

x Sunday only.   *Bus.

SACRAMENTO NORTHERN

Low Round Trip Fares

EVEN AS LATE AS November 19, 1939, the Sacramento Northern issued a timetable making it appear to be a busy interurban line. This schedule does not show additional trains to Concord and Pittsburg. It also offers no hint of the dwindling patronage that was plaguing the company despite efforts to attract new riders with service on the new Bay Bridge tracks directly into San Francisco. The heyday of electric interurban service was over and nothing could bring it back. The service was drastically cut back in 1940 and, except for streetcar service in Sacramento, Marysville-Yuba City and Chico, was abandoned in 1941. The SN operated a limited bus service, below, to supplement rail service and to keep competing bus operators from gaining operating rights on roads parallel to the rail line. The dark green interurban car and snazzy ACF-Brill bus offered quite a contrast in 1940 at Pittsburg. Unlike many interurbans, SN did not stay in the bus business after discontinuing rail operation but sold its vehicles and routes to operators such as Greyhound.

*Timetable, John K. Kelly Collection;
photo, Waldemar Sievers*

ON OPENING DAY, April 25, 1906, Northern Electric 101 awaits the signal to depart Chico for Oroville. Car 100 was the first car to make the journey. An open streetcar that also carried celebrants is on the left. The 101 also made the last trip from Sacramento to Chico on October 31, 1940. Five NE cars are posed, right, in Chico in 1917. The first car, the 127, was built by the Northern Electric following the design of other cars built by the Niles Car & Manufacturing Company, which built the 101.

Above, Harre W. Demoro Collection; below, L. L. Bonney Collection

GRACEFULLY PROPORTIONED wooden cars were a characteristic of the lines north of Sacramento, which used 600-volt third rail except in cities, where a trolley pole was necessary. On this page, the 101, built in 1906 by Niles Car & Manufacturing, rolls past Thermalito station on the Oroville Branch about 1915. The station was a standard NE design. Below, one of the wooden cars delivered in 1906 by Cincinnati Car Company awaits passengers at Colusa, also on a branch line, in 1920. On the opposite page, the 109, which was built in 1906 by St. Louis Car Company for the Philadelphia & Western (see San Francisco "Subs," page 40), rolls into Meridian on a Colusa-Marysville branch run on January 2, 1940. Below, the squarish appearance of four ex-P&W cars and the more graceful 127, built by NE following Niles plans, can be compared at Marysville in 1939. Almost identical cars similar to NE's Niles interurbans also were used by the Napa Valley (pages 114-119).

This page, Harre W. Demoro Collection;
opposite, top, Ted Wurm; below, Dudley Thickens

UNION STATION in Sacramento, California's capital city, was the meeting place of the ex-Northern Electric and former San Francisco-Sacramento Railroad (OA&E) lines. For a few years it was also used by the Sacramento-Stockton cars of the Central California Traction. The squarish 1014 on the left, above, is assigned to the 1,200-volt Sacramento-San Francisco line, while the arch-windowed 220 and 127 are in 600-volt Sacramento-Woodland service. In the final months of Woodland and Sacramento-Chico service, the larger but plainer cars from the San Francisco predecessor were assigned to Woodland and Chico service. They were faster than the old Northern Electric equipment; also, they could operate on both 600 and 1,200 volts, and were equipped with pole trolleys and third rail shoes as well as pantographs (for running on the Key System and the Bay Bridge). Trains from San Francisco shared the monumental M Street Bridge, left, with Sacramento-Woodland trains. The 1009 is on Train 2, *The Comet*, which left San Francisco at 8:03 A.M., and will pull into Union Station at 10:50 A.M., seven minutes after the picture was taken. On the page opposite, top, the 1003, on *The Comet* en route to San Francisco, has just exited SN's mile-long tunnel and is whistling past Havens station high in the Oakland hills. Park Boulevard is at the right. Below, on January 14, 1939, the SN ran a special train to ceremonies marking the completion of the tracks on the San Francisco-Oakland Bay Bridge.

Opposite, below, Vernon J. Sappers Collection
others, Waldemar Sievers

THE OAKLAND, Antioch & Eastern Railway was never able to complete a bridge across the Sacramento and San Joaquin Rivers between Mallard and Chipps, so entire trains had to be transported by ferry. San Francisco-bound 1014, opposite, top, departs the gasoline-driven ferry, *Ramon*, in 1940. Because the OA&E also couldn't afford to buy much property in Oakland, its yard at 40th Street and Shafter Avenue was compact. An unusual three-way switch, below, was used in the "Back Shop."

Two of SN's four parlor-observation cars are featured on this page. The *Moraga*, above, is on a railroad enthusiast's special at its namesake station, Moraga, about 1940. Below, the *Bidwell*, built by the Northern Electric from a wrecked Niles-built car, decorates the rear of a train at Marysville in 1939.

Opposite, top, Waldemar Sievers; below, Ralph W. Demoro;
this page, top, Waldemar Sievers; below, Dudley Thickens

FREIGHT SERVICE was important to the Sacramento Northern from its earliest days. The promoters of its predecessor companies realized that the passenger traffic for which most U.S. interurbans were built would be insufficient. The Northern Electric built the 82-ton 1010 in 1911 to both carry freight and pull freight trains, while the Oakland, Antioch & Eastern acquired the 601 (originally 101) from American Car Company in 1912 to carry passengers and freight, and to pull freight and passenger trains. The car, shown below at Fairfield in 1930, had seats that could be folded down for passengers. On the page opposite, the 62-ton steeple-cab 652, built by General Electric in 1928, pauses in 1957 at Walnut Creek, approximately where a rapid transit station would be opened in 1973. Conductor Walter Butterfield, left, and motorman O. H. Schindler, posed in the cab of motor 653 a few days before the 38-mile Oakland-Pittsburg electric freight service was discontinued in February 1957.   *Above, L. L. Bonney Collection;*
below, Ralph W. Demoro; opposite, Harre W. Demoro

Redwood Empire Electrics

WHEN JOHN MARTIN and Eugene de Sabla decided in 1902 to electrify their narrow-gauged commuter trains in Marin County, the technology was brand new and some of it had never been applied to an electric railway. The North Shore took the 600-volt third rail system already proven on elevated lines in New York, Chicago and Boston, and General Electric equipment that had been successful in elevated rapid transit service, and installed it on a busy steam-operated railroad, which was altered for both narrow- and standard-gauged trains. So many trains were to be operated that a new type of signaling system had to be developed, one that would not interfere with the electrical power system. The result is shown above, the first steam railroad electrified for efficiency of operation rather than to solve terminal congestion or to eliminate smoke. The wooden train is on the curve leading to Mill Valley in August 1903, when the line opened. On the page opposite, top, one of the modern cars acquired in 1929-30 stops at Ross, one of the area's wealthiest communities, in 1938. Below, a train headed to Fairfax and Manor screeches around the curve at San Anselmo in 1939. The tower controlled the junction between the Manor and San Rafael lines. The building with the arched window was an electrical substation.   *Above, Vernon J. Sappers Collection; opposite, top, Charles A. Smallwood; below, Ralph W. Demoro*

UNTIL THE NORTH SHORE, few electric railroads had signaling systems; standard designs using direct current in the track to trigger the signals would interfere with the negative circuit also in the track that returned the electricity to the powerhouse or substation. The Union Switch & Signal Co. developed a system using alternating current circuits that, after being proven on the North Shore, was adopted for rapid transit and other high-speed electric railways. On the page opposite, the signal points up for Proceed (the train is approaching on the other track and not affected by the signal). A minute later a Sausalito-bound train passes and the signal drops to Stop in the photo below. On this page, NWP 312, delivered to the railroad in 1908 by St. Louis Car Co., was photographed at Manor in 1938. The front of one of these wooden cars is shown below at Pine Yard at Sausalito. The North Shore painted the wooden cars red but NWP repainted them Pullman green.

Both pages, Ralph W. Demoro

ALMOST THE ENTIRE history of the Mill Valley Branch is depicted on the page opposite. Above, captured in 1911 on a glass plate negative, a Mill Valley-bound train occupies the single-track curve from the main line at right. The electric third rail was left unprotected at most locations but has a safety cover here because the location is a station. The same junction is shown below, on September 29, 1940; two days later the line would be abandoned except for school train service. The entire

NWP electrification was disconnected on March 1, 1941. The new cars built of steel and aluminum delivered in 1929-30 by St. Louis Car Co. are shown on this page. They were sent to the Pacific Electric Railway during World War II and one survived to be on the very last PE train in 1961.

Opposite, top, Vernon J. Sappers Collection;
below, Ted Wurm; above, Charles A. Smallwood;
below, Ralph W. Demoro

MOMENTS AFTER THE ferry arrived at Sausalito, commuters rushed to the waiting suburban trains. The big pumpkin-orange electrics were near the end of their Marin careers in 1940. NWP electric trains carried the same oil marker lights at the rear as did the steam trains calling at Sausalito. Both steam and electric crews alike were governed by a strict rulebook and the men were all on the same seniority list. Those with enough years would work on the electrics in the winter and the steam trains in the summer. A bottleneck left over from the steam suburban train days was the narrow, single-tracked tunnel, left, under Alto Hill south of Corte Madera. The Golden Gate Bridge, opened in 1937, doomed the trains and ferries.

Above, Vernon J. Sappers Collection;
left, Waldemar Sievers

THE NEW COMMUTER cars acquired in 1929-30 by NWP could really pack in the passengers with their three-two seating arrangement. The rods and dials in the ceiling were for the Ohmer fare register on the bulkhead to the right of the door. The cars seated either 98 or 103 passengers, depending on whether they had a smoking section. NWP 354, below, one of the original cars delivered in 1902-03 by the St. Louis Car Company, was still in service in 1937, with glistening new paint.

Above, Vernon J. Sappers; below, Waldemar Sievers

Electric Traction's New Era

WHEN VOTERS APPROVED, in November 1962, the bond issue to construct the Bay Area Rapid Transit system, a lot of people figured the hard part was over. In retrospect, winning support from voters was the easiest task. Building BART was tough, sometimes a nightmare, as when funds almost ran out in 1966 because of inflation spurred by the Vietnam War. Some of the people who participated in BART's early history are on these two pages. Opposite, two workers wrestle with an air-operated tool in a downtown Oakland subway tunnel in 1968. On this page, above, the date is June 19, 1964, and BART General Manager B. R. Stokes, center, is flanked by President Lyndon Johnson and U.S. Senator Pierre Salinger, right, at groundbreaking for the test track that was built from Concord to Walnut Creek. At right, President and Mrs. Richard M. Nixon exit a BART train with Stokes on September 27, 1972, about two weeks after the Fremont-MacArthur line opened on September 11. Despite its many embarrassing and much-publicized problems, BART trains were carrying about 215,000 weekday riders in 1985. The prototypes of 150 cars on order from Alsthom Atlantique, a French builder, arrived by ship in San Francisco on August 24, 1985, and several areas without BART service were investigating ways to finance extensions for completion in the 21st century.

Opposite, BART; this page, above, Lonnie Wilson, Oakland
Tribune; *below, Gordon Kloess—BART*

ONCE A LAWSUIT to block BART was dismissed in 1964, construction and testing began. On November 15, 1969, most of the structural work had been completed at the Hayward elevated station, above. Some of the third rail was still scattered alongside the tracks, and insulators and coverboards remained to be installed, along with automatic train control and the decorative covering on passenger platforms. The first of three laboratory cars acquired in March 1965 to test new components on the Diablo Test Track between Concord and Walnut Creek was being checked out prior to its first run on April 12, 1965. Opposite, Lab Car B scoots under the Oak Grove School overpass on the test track in March 1966; below, Car C, cut down so it would fit in subway tunnels, is at Hayward in 1970 to test automatic control equipment. *All, Harre W. Demoro*

THE FIRST PROTOTYPE passenger car, BART's 101, arrived at Hayward Shop on August 28, 1970, and was unveiled the following day. Of the 10 prototypes (101-107, 501-503) only 107 and 501-503 were refitted for passenger service. Cars 103 and 105 were wrecked at Coliseum station during testing and were not replaced by production cars. The 101, 102, 104 and 106 were scrapped and replaced by production cars. Prototype 101 was not complete when delivered by Rohr Industries Incorporated. Among the items it lacked was automatic train control equipment. Above, the car rests in the Hayward Shop before being pushed outside to greet reporters and district officials. Left, BART publicist P.O. Ormsbee, who later became the district secretary, inspects the intercar closure. The 101 was closer to the ground than usual because air springs were deflated. On the page opposite are views of the control console of the first production cars and the interior of the cars as delivered without ceiling handholds, which were added later.

All, Harre W. Demoro

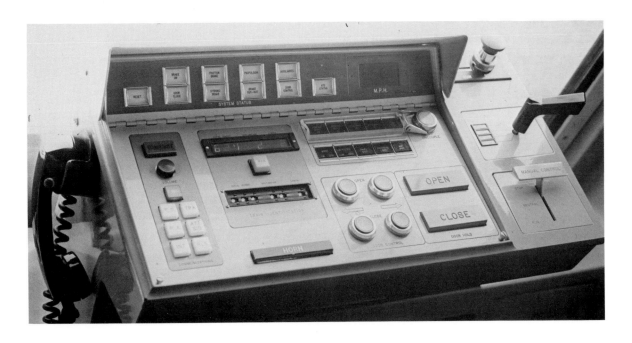

AS OPENING DAY APPROACHED, it was becoming obvious to BART officials that fewer than 20 cars would be ready for passengers on September 11, 1972. These photos were taken at Hayward Yard just before opening day. Above, four glistening new A cars await a final inspection on September 9. Below, in a view from the yard tower, fewer than 25 cars are in the yard on September 10, the day before service began. On the page opposite, the Hayward towerman on September 10 punches a route into the console for a test train entering the yard from Fremont that had broken down several times that afternoon.

All, Harre W. Demoro

THE 71-MILE BART system runs underground, on viaducts and at ground level, with the types of construction evenly divided in thirds. On the page opposite, top, both the concrete ties on the ballasted surface main line and wooden ties at switches are shown with the steel and aluminum 1,000-volt third rail east of Rockridge station. The graceful concrete elevated structure at the Bay Fair station is below. On this page,

above, an Oakland-bound train pauses in the crossover between North Berkeley and Berkeley stations. Below, a Fremont-bound BART train passes a Western Pacific Railroad freight drag in Oakland, offering an example of how BART designers minimized disruption by combining transport systems into one corridor. *Both pages, Harre W. Demoro*

Grape-Hauler And Traction On the Coast

THE SMALLEST ELECTRIC railway operation in the state was the electrified industrial switching line at Winehaven on San Pablo Bay (near the Richmond dock of the automobile ferry line to San Rafael). The California Wine Association built a short electric line from a wharf on San Pablo Bay, where riverboats loaded with grapes were docked, to its winery ashore. Few photographs were taken of the Winehaven trains and most of them, such as the view at left, taken in the late 1930s, show the line's locomotives after operations had ceased. The locomotive was acquired in 1922 from another obscure electric line, the hard-luck Ocean Shore Railroad, which was supposed to be a high-speed electric interurban line linking San Francisco with the resort city of Santa Cruz. The Ocean Shore built south from San Francisco to Tunitas below Half Moon Bay and north from Santa Cruz to Swanton, but never connected the two sections. The line, dealt a fiscal blow by the 1906 earthquake — which severely damaged the tracks — was operated by steam power until abandonment in 1920, except for a portion of its route in San Francisco. On the page opposite, electric motor 51 was switching rock bunkers shortly before the line was abandoned, and in the lower view, the same motor is shown near Army Street. It is believed that the Petaluma & Santa Rosa Railroad salvaged parts from Ocean Shore 51 to build its 506.

This page, Ted Wurm; opposite, above, Rudolph Brandt Collection; below, Bert Ward Collection.

Out Where Grass Begins

When the whole world just seems to radiate heat, there is solace in the country---out where the air is pure and sweet---you will find nature awaiting you with a smile.

For a little while just leave behind the worry; get away from worry and hum-drum to the delightful recreation that the woods and fields afford.   You'll go back better fitted for the wrangle of life.

GO ON AN INTERURBAN RIDE TO-NIGHT.

Petaluma and Santa Rosa Railroad Company

Interurban To World's Egg Basket

EGGS WERE A MAJOR industry in Sonoma County by 1900 and there were more hens than people in Petaluma and vicinity when the Petaluma & Santa Rosa Railroad began laying track and stringing wire in 1904, part of a scheme by local merchants and ranchers to challenge the monopoly of the San Francisco & North Pacific Railroad (also called the California Northwestern and ultimately the Northwestern Pacific). P&SR wooed passengers and freight with—for their time—clever advertising, such as the message, above, which was placed in frames specially installed on car bulkheads for promotional purposes. On the page opposite are scenes the interurban management did not have in mind when it decided to compete for business against the California Northwestern. What would soon be known in local lore as "the battle of Sebastapol Avenue" was waged between the P&SR and CNW in 1905 when the electric road attempted to cross the steam line in Santa Rosa. A great and most entertaining battle that drew a huge crowd occurred in March of that year when locomotives spraying steam on P&SR track crews managed to delay installation of the crossing, as shown in the upper view. But the fisticuffs didn't last long and the interurban prevailed, as shown in the bottom frame, with electric car, happy officials and employees, and the crossover in the foreground. P&SR linked its namesake cities and also had branches to Two Rock and Forestville. A steamer calling at Petaluma was the San Francisco connection. At its peak, the line was 37 miles long.   *Above, Harre W. Demoro Collection, opposite, L. L. Bonney Collection*

P&SR ONLY ASSIGNED odd numbers to its passenger cars, so it might appear that the interurban road's equipment roster was much larger than the actual total of 10 cars. Six of the cars, 59-69, were delivered by the San Francisco builder, Holman, in 1904 and were of the conventional interurban design with end doors and interior compartments for baggage-express, smoking passengers and non-smokers. The cars originally were painted a chocolate color but soon white was applied, only to be discontinued in favor of yellow, because motorists could not tell the difference between a speeding electric interurban car and the hundreds of white-colored chicken coops along the tracks through the "Egg Basket of the World." Car 65, above, in Santa Rosa about 1920, is in white livery, but the 63, below, in Sebastapol about 1905, has the original chocolate scheme. To the left is one of the P&SR's fearsome-looking "Windsplitter" cars.

Above, Vernon J. Sappers Collection;
below, Charles Smallwood Collection

Sebastopol

THE "WINDSPLITTERS" were among the most unusual inter-urban cars to operate in the far west, and their origin is something of a mystery. Although they are shown in a catalog of the John Stephenson Company of Elizabeth, New Jersey, some records indicate the cars were built by the American Car Company in St. Louis. Both builders were subsidiaries of Philadelphia-based J.G. Brill Company in 1904 when P&SR bought the cars, which had been exhibited at the St. Louis World's Fair, and had won their builder a medal for workmanship and design. The four cars apparently were intended for single-ended running, because they had a fancy enclosed observation compart-

ment. Nevertheless, that probably was considered excessive in rural Sonoma County and P&SR put controls on the back and ran the cars as double-enders. Below, in original chocolate paint, the 53 posed about 1905 on Sebastapol Avenue in Santa Rosa. The 51, above, on 4th Street in Santa Rosa about 1920, is painted white. The unusual center door was not found on most interurbans, but the rounded ends were repeated on cars built of steel some years later as part of a largely unsuccessful effort in the east and midwest to save energy by "streamlining."

Above, Charles A. Smallwood Collection;
below, L. L. Bonney Collection

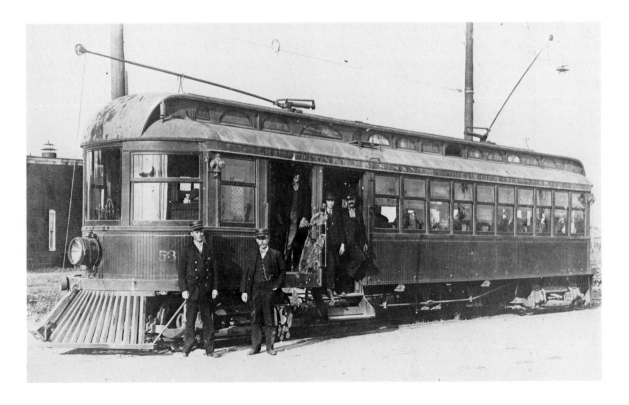

MOST INTERURBANS WERE built for passenger trains but the P&SR bought four freight motors in 1904 and emphasized freight service as well as passengers. Its owners intended to compete against the steam railroad and owned a steamboat to haul both freight and passengers from Petaluma to San Francisco. One of the original freight motors is shown, opposite, top, in Sebastapol, with a long train of flatcars loaded with debris or rock. This could be a construction train or, as suggested by some historians, it may be a load of debris being hauled from Santa Rosa after the Great Earthquake of April 18, 1906. Another original locomotive, the 1004, was rebuilt in the 1920s and lasted until 1947 when the P&SR was converted to diesel. It is shown, opposite, below, coupled to a booster unit, a flatcar equipped with electric motors. On this page, above,

P&SR 502, ex-Kansas City, Kaw Valley & Western, was placed on a trestle for publicity purposes shortly after it was acquired in 1920. The ungainly unit below is P&SR's portable substation, which was mounted on a flatcar so it could be moved over the line to supply power as needed when traffic shifted. Several other California interurbans used portable substations, including the Pacific Electric and Sacramento Northern. Southern Pacific through its Northwestern Pacific subsidiary bought the P&SR in 1932 and passenger service ended that year. The railroad itself was abandoned in 1984.

Opposite, above, L. L. Bonney Collection;
below, both pages, Milliard Brown;
above, Vernon J. Sappers Collection

Trains to the Valley of The Geysers

BY 1900 THE FERTILE Napa Valley north of San Francisco had become both lush vineyard country and a major destination for vacationers. Persons suffering from ill health thrived in the dry summer heat and bathed in the many hot springs that bubbled from the ground—including some that were large enough to be considered geysers. The Vallejo, Benicia & Napa Valley Railroad was built, starting in 1905, to compete against the Southern Pacific for the business, and was electrified with the unusual alternating current system, first at 750 volts and later at 3,300 volts. On the page opposite, above, a steel car originally built in 1910 for another AC road, the Visalia Electric,

awaits departure with a trailing railway post office car at the Vallejo ferry wharf in 1937, shortly before passenger service ceased. Car 47 on the page opposite and the car at the bottom of this page were among the interurbans acquired in 1905 to open the line. A construction train is shown above. The line never reached Benicia, but was built between Vallejo, Napa and Calistoga, and had several names in its unstable history. The Monticello (later Golden Gate Ferry and finally Southern Pacific Golden Gate Ferry) provided the electric line's San Francisco connection.

Opposite, Ted Wurm; this page, Bert Ward Collection

GRACEFUL WOODEN CARS built by Niles Car & Manufacturing Company—following the same plans of Northern Electric Railway—were the Napa Valley Route's mainstay in its middle years, when thousands of passengers streamed off the Monticello Steamship vessels at Vallejo and boarded the trains for Napa and Calistoga. The Niles cars are shown on this page in their early years and, opposite, bottom, in the mid-1930s when steel cars took what little business was left. The steel car on the page opposite is one of two obtained in 1933 to replace cars lost in a carbarn fire in 1932. These were the last traditional interurban cars built in the United States and only ran as electric railway cars for less than five years.

This page, Bert Ward Collection; opposite, W. Silverthorn

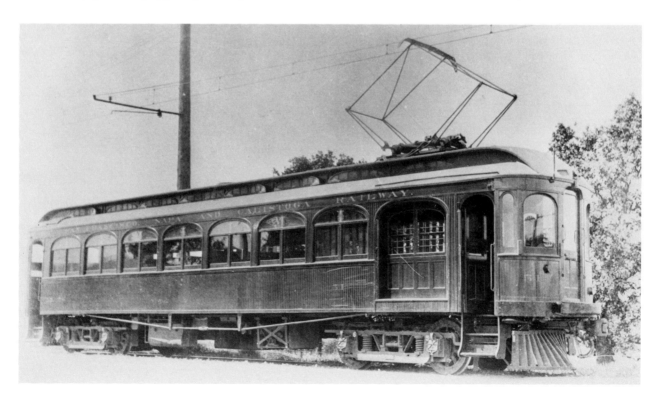

TRAGEDY STALKED the Napa Valley. The worst interurban wreck in California history occurred on the line on June 19, 1913, when 13 persons were killed in a head-on collision north of Vallejo. The wreck bankrupted the interurban line. On January 22, 1932, a fire gutted the powerhouse and carbarn at Napa, below, also destroying three cars and shutting down the line until May 29, when limited service was restored. Most freight handled by the road originated at the huge Mare Island Naval Shipyard at Vallejo and motor 99, page opposite, was built in 1922 (with assistance of the Sacramento Northern) for the military traffic. In the bottom photo, two styles of interurban architecture can be compared, the straightforward steel car and graceful wooden construction.

This page, Bert Ward Collection;
opposite, top, Harre W. Demoro Collection;
below, Waldemar Sievers

Blossom Trolleyland

EARLY IN THE 20th century, Santa Clara County—the Silicon Valley of the 1980s—was called "The Valley of the Heart's Delight," so wonderful was its soil, weather and physical location. Expecting big profits, Southern Pacific merged the street railway system into San Jose Railroads; it also created the Peninsular Railway out of several existing lines, continued new construction and sponsored the Blossom Trolley Trip through the orchards. The streetcars ran until 1938 and always struggled, and the Peninsular lost money for 16 consecutive years from 1919 to 1934. The variety of San Jose equipment is evident on these two pages. A red Peninsular car with air whistle on its roof, left, pauses in downtown San Jose in the 1920s while in Bascome interurban service. One of the big double-truck "California Type" cars bought by Peninsular from American Car Company in 1912 for San Jose Railroads was on the Willows line, opposite above, in 1915. Like most small town systems, San Jose had Birney cars. Yellow SJRR 139, below, was built by St. Louis Car Company in 1920. A light rail line is scheduled to bring back San Jose's trolley era in a modern form in the late 1980s.

Left and opposite above, Charles A. Smallwood; below, Douglas Richter

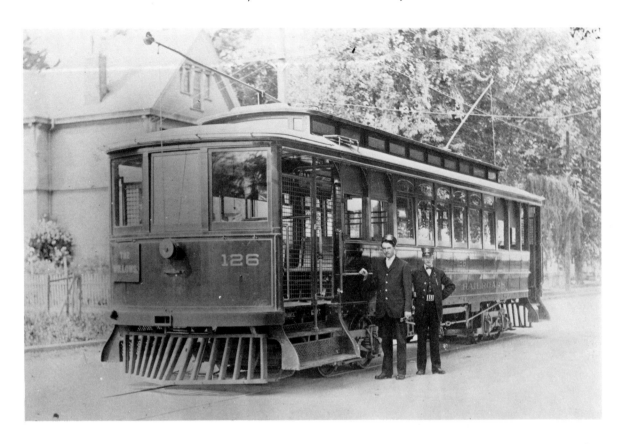

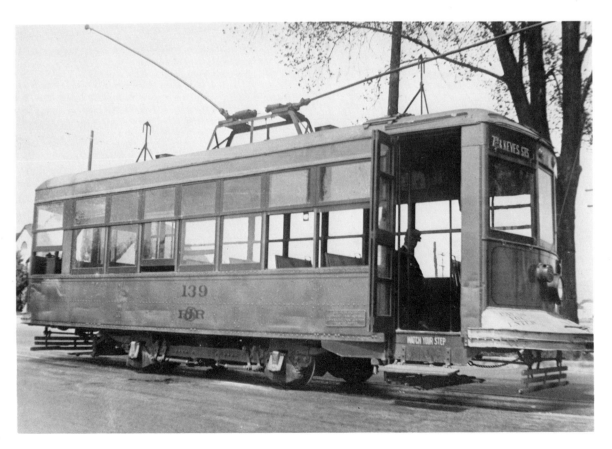

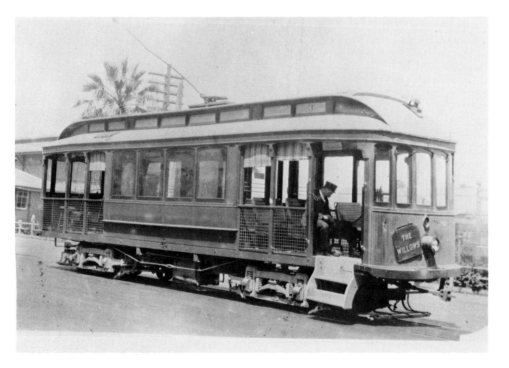

THE "CALIFORNIA TYPE" car with enclosed center and open ends was popular in warm San Jose. The car below was built in 1902 by American Car Company for the Los Angeles Pacific Railway, which later came under Southern Pacific control and was merged into the Pacific Electric in 1911. The car came to the Peninsular in 1923, which numbered it 32. San Francisco-based Holman manufactured San Jose-Los Gatos Interurban Railway 16, above, in 1905. This car was absorbed into the Peninsular Railway roster and ran until 1930. Peninsular also ran streetcars in Palo Alto.

Above, Robert McFarland, below, Charles A. Smallwood Collection

THE RELOCATION of the Southern Pacific main line through San Jose in the 1930s resulted in the construction of several underpasses. San Jose Railroads 77, operating on East Santa Clara Street, ducks under the tracks while en route to King Road, on April 1, 1938. An example of how San Jose Railroads and Peninsular swapped cars is shown below. Peninsular 71 was built in 1913 by Jewett for San Jose Railroads, but sent to Peninsular service in 1927 as a Comfort Car on the San Jose-Los Gatos line to replace the 50-type cars, which were being retired. However, the 50s soon were returned to service after being converted to one-man cars because the Comfort Cars hardly lived up to their name. The 71 was sent back to SJRR in 1933.

Above, Charles A. Smallwood;
below, Harre W. Demoro Collection

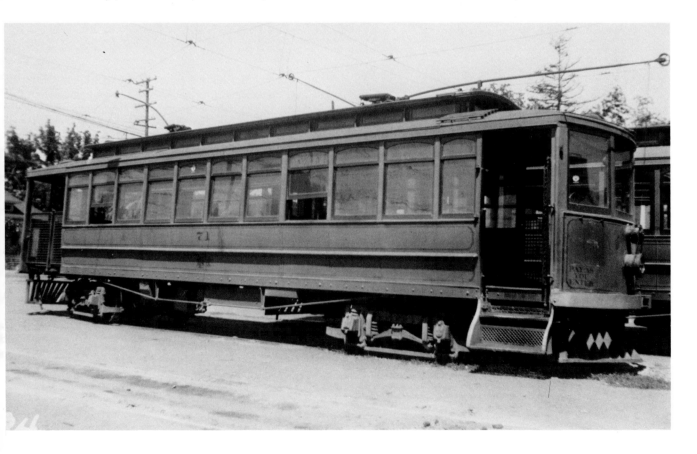

SAN JOSE'S PREMIER electric railway cars were the eight "Big Pallies," nicknamed for their size and assignment to San Jose-Palo Alto service. The wood and steel cars were part of an order for 53 cars built in 1913 by Jewett at Newark, Ohio, for the Pacific Electric (which numbered its 45 cars 1000-1044) and the Peninsular, which assigned the cars numbers 105-112. All 53 cars were capable of either 600-or 1,200-volt operation (Peninsular was only 600) and were quite fast, good for 60 miles an hour and more on good track. On the page opposite, Peninsular 111 was posed on the San Jose-Palo Alto line between Meridian and Monte Vista to promote the candidacy of motorman L.J. Edwards, who was seeking election about 1925 as an official of the trainmen's union. Edwards later became a Key System motorman in Oakland, and cars 105-112 were put in storage until 1937 when PE rehabilitated them as PE 1050-1057. Also on these pages are two scenes of San Jose Railroads streetcars just prior to abandonment in 1938. The upper view is of a Berryessa car on East Santa Clara Street, and the frame opposite shows a San Jose-Santa Clara car on The Alameda.

Right, Vernon J. Sappers Collection;
others, Waldemar Sievers

PENINSULAR'S "STANDARD" interurban cars were the trim 50-type, built in 1903 by American Car Company for the San Jose & Los Gatos Interurban as 2-13. Originally, half were motor cars and half were unpowered trailers, but eventually all were motorized. Weighing 27 tons and being 45 feet long, they were typical interurbans of the era, except for their 8-feet three-inch width, unusually narrow and leading to incorrect reports many years ago that they were originally intended for a narrow-gauged line. The cars were finished with etched upper windows and interiors trimmed with cherry. On the page opposite are views of the 50 type in their prime. The trestle (replaced about 1912) was between Saratoga and Los Gatos and shows how rural the countryside was in the era of the interurban. In the view below, the bright red 59, trimmed in gold leaf, is at East Santa Clara and 17th streets en route to Alum Rock Park in the 1920s. Because of their two-man crews, the 50s were costly to operate and Peninsular put them in storage in 1928 in favor of the so-called "Comfort Cars" of the 70 series, which were un-popular. Management reluctantly returned the 50s to service in 1930 after rebuilding them for one-man service. The cars in their final days are shown on this page, the red and cream 60 awaiting passengers at the SP station in 1930 and, right, the 58, carrying a dash sign reading, "San Jose, Saratoga, Los Gatos."

Opposite, top, Charles A. Smallwood Collection;
below, Vernon J. Sappers Collection;
above, Ralph W. Demoro; below, J. C. Gordon

Traction in the High Sierra

THE NEVADA COUNTY Traction Company, which commenced service between Grass Valley and Nevada City in the gold country of the Sierra Nevada in 1901, was promoted by John Martin and Eugene de Sabla, who were to electrify the North Shore Railroad in Marin County in 1903, and earn lasting fame as founders of the huge Pacific Gas and Electric Company. On the page opposite, a crowd has swarmed aboard what might be one of the first cars over the line; below, on a street free of automobiles, the number 4 awaits passengers in Grass Valley. The three-stall carbarn is shown above and, below, a car shares Broad Street in Nevada City with motor vehicles in the early 1920s. The 4½-mile line never reopened after a severe snowstorm in 1924.   *Two top photos, Grahame Hardy Collection; others, Al Phelps Collection*

Traction in the Great Valley

CALIFORNIA'S GREAT Central Valley extends for 400 miles. In the north it is called the Sacramento Valley, and in the south, the San Joaquin Valley, the names deriving from the principal river systems through the great basin, which is among the most fertile areas on earth. By the dawn of the 20th century, railroads and the beginnings of irrigation had made valley farmers wealthy and transformed dusty towns into prosperous cities large enough for street railways. The capital city of Sacramento was the hub of valley traction, having the Sacramento Northern and Central California Traction Company, Union Station and three street-car companies. On the page opposite, a Sacramento City Lines car passed the Capitol in 1946. North from the capital city, the Sacramento Northern was the principal electric railway (pages 76-87). To the south, several companies were active, including, above, Southern Pacific-owned Stockton Electric, which had Hedley-Doyle Stepless Cars (or Dragons) in the 1920s, and the trolley and third rail Central California Traction, below, which hauled freight behind a variety of box motors.

Opposite and below, Ralph W. Demoro;
above, Charles A. Smallwood Collection

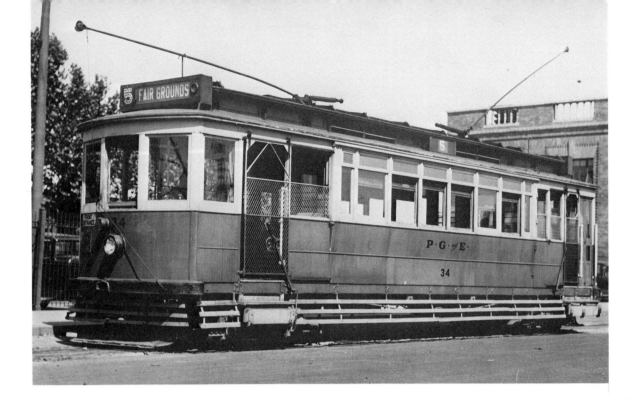

SACRAMENTO'S DRY and hot summer weather made the "California Type" car especially popular in the early days. On the page opposite, the Pacific Gas and Electric's barn at 26th Street was photographed about 1915 by the company photographer. The automobile in the center of the photo is a sample of what was to come. Above, predecessor Sacramento Electric Gas & Railway Company 103 carried advertisements for John Breuner, a pioneer Northern California furniture store. On this page, a PG&E car built in the company shops picked its way past flivver traffic on J Street, below, in 1920. Above, a similar car considerably rebuilt and now with a one-man crew was awaiting passengers in 1935 at the new Southern Pacific station.

Above, Harre W. Demoro Collection;
opposite, below, PG&E;
this page, above, Ralph W. Demoro;
below, Vernon J. Sappers Collection

PG&E GOT ITS money's worth out of its old cars, rebuilding them from two-man to one-man operation by enclosing ends and adding folding doors and steps. The 18, above, at the SP depot in 1938, had been modified several times. Aside from little Birney cars, which first appeared in 1918, Sacramento's first modern steel cars were five lightweight streetcars acquired in 1924 from American Car Company. As shown below, these cars had large windows and big roof destination signs. On the page opposite is a mixture of old and new in the PG&E carbarn in 1938 and a lineup of PG&E's two lightweight styles at the carbarn in 1946. The 62, opposite, was a "Christmas Present Car," one of 12 cars built in 1929 by American Car Company and introduced to the public on Christmas Day.

Opposite, above, Ralph W. Demoro;
below, Waldemar Sievers;
above, Waldemar Sievers; below, Ralph W. Demoro

FRESNO TRACTION COMPANY, a Southern Pacific subsidiary, bought 12 double-truck Birney cars from St. Louis Car Company in 1925 that had careers elsewhere after Fresno's street railway went into decline. Fresno 87, page opposite, above, was among nine of the cars sold in 1939 to the Central California Traction Company (owned one-third each by SP, Santa Fe and Western Pacific), which used them in Sacramento, as shown page opposite, below. CCT 88 is passing CCT box motor 7 at the company's X and Alhambra streets yard about 1940. The box motor was secondhand, too, having been built originally for the Washington, Baltimore & Annapolis. The CCT cars went to Sacramento City Lines in 1944 when CCT sold out to the new bus-oriented company, which also bought the Sacramento Northern and PG&E streetcar operations. City Lines junked the rail routes in 1947, shortly after the photos on this page were taken of the ex-Fresno cars. In 1933, three other Fresno cars became Pacific Electric 150-152.

Opposite, above, Bert Ward; below, Charles A. Smallwood; this page, Ralph W. Demoro

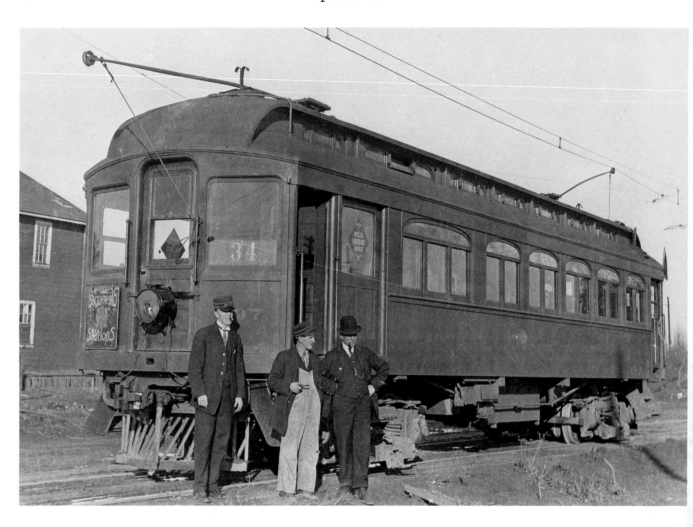

THE 53-MILE main line of the Central California Traction Company linked California's capital with Stockton, the principal port on the San Joaquin River and a great agricultural center. Car 207, one of the four Holman-built interurbans acquired for the opening of the main line in 1910, was on train 34 at Stockton about 1920, which made the 53-mile journey in one hour and 50 minutes. Note the third rail shoes, which were used outside cities on the CCT. The company had an unusual third rail design with the shoe rubbing on the bottom of the rail. The road also was among the first to adopt General Electric's 1,200-volt system. CCT was quick to promote to special events, such as an aviation meet April 19-20, 1912, at the State Fairgrounds. *Above, Charles A. Smallwood; left, Harre W. Demoro Collection*

CCT'S FIRST INTERURBANS were four cars built in 1906 by American Car Company for Stockton-Lodi service, which began in 1907. The cars, considered noteworthy enough to be illustrated in the August 1910 J.G. Brill Company catalog, originally had both open and closed sections and were similar to Pacific Electric's 800-type cars. One of the cars survived the abandonment of passenger service in 1933 as, above, locomotive 1. The Holman-built cars were considered the premier cars by the company. Two of them were posed, below, for publicity purposes along the Sacramento-Stockton main line about 1910. There were eight round trips daily between Stockton and Sacramento in 1920. *Above, Harre W. Demoro Collection; below, Arthur L. Lloyd Collection*

THE TRACTION COMPANY operated streetcars in Stockton from 1906 to 1914 and in Sacramento from 1910 to 1944. The Stockton lines were merged into SP's Stockton Electric system when the steam railroad gained control (which the government later forced it to share with Santa Fe and Western Pacific) of the CCT. The Sacramento line was operated to satisfy franchise requirements relating to CCT's interurban line to Stockton and was sold to Sacramento City Lines in 1944. The Sacramento line ran from downtown Sacramento to Colonial Heights and was the most convenient way to reach the baseball park, where the Pacific Coast League Solons played for some years. The 101, above, at Colonial Heights in the 1930s, was built by St. Louis Car Company in 1906 for Stockton Electric. While the street cars were money losers, the freight scene below would warm an accountant's heart. Box motor 3 is switching a packing house in Stockton about 1940. *Both, Charles A. Smallwood*

STOCKTON RODE the crest of California's agricultural boom; its population swelled from 23,000 in 1910 to 40,000 in 1920, and to 48,000 in 1930. SP-owned Stockton Electric Railroad had two eras. The early period used wooden cars such as the 23-28 type, below, passing the San Joaquin County Court House in 1920. This general style of car was phased out in the late 1920s (some went to SP-owned San Jose Railroads) as enough Birney cars, such as the 63 above, were available. The 63 was among six Birneys acquired secondhand from San Diego Electric in 1925. In 1931, Stockton Electric operated 40 passenger streetcars and two work cars over 24.37 miles of track. The fare was seven cents and patrons could buy four tokens for a quarter. *Above, Waldemar Sievers; below, R. T. Hill*

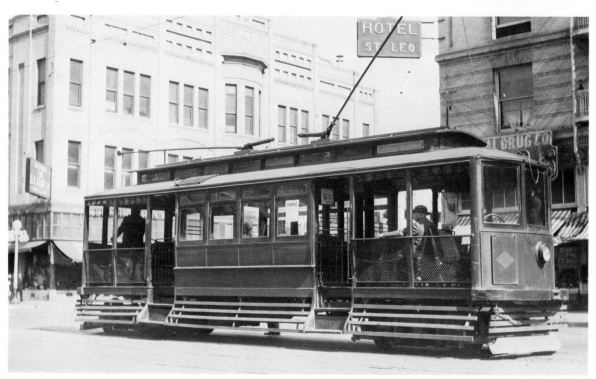

TWO REMARKABLE photographs taken when amateur cameras and film were primitive capture the atmosphere of Stockton's streetcars on February 4, 1940. Both pictures were taken aboard Birney car 64 on Ophir Street. Note the simple, hard seats, farebox with transfers, and polished metal seat handles. In the view below, car 58 is seen through the rear window of 64 on East Main crossing Ophir. On the page opposite are three pre-Birney era views in Stockton. The car in the bottom view is a Hedley-Doyle Stepless Car, also called a Hobbleskirt Car, or Dragon, that was unbearable to ride in Stockton's blistering summer heat. It was sent to the Pacific Electric and used in Long Beach. SP sold Stockton Electric to Pacific City Lines on April 1, 1939. The new company abandoned rail service in favor of buses between October 1940 and September 1941.

Opposite, R. T. Hill; this page, Ted Wurm

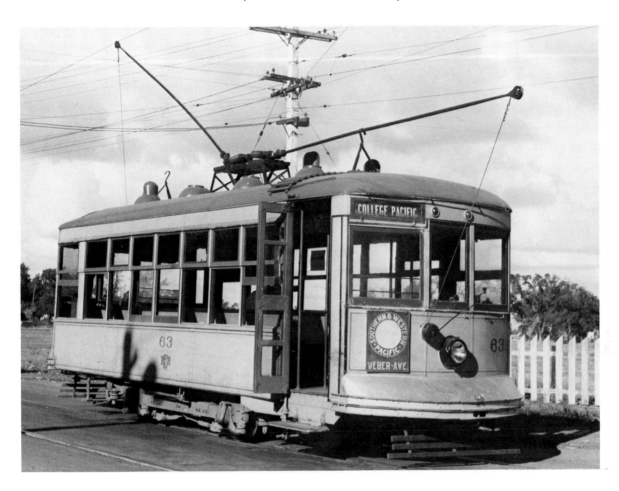

THE ORNATE Hotel Stockton, page opposite, top, was a traction hub in the days when the Central California Traction Company and Tidewater Southern used it as an interurban station. All that ran on the Main Street track in 1939 were Stockton Electric's little Birney cars. Railfans chartered car 63, shown opposite below at the carbarn and above, this page, just before service was discontinued in 1940-41. In the view below, car 46 has stopped at the end of the California Street line at Alpine Avenue. Oak Park is in the background.

Below, Ted Wurm; others, Waldemar Sievers

THE TIDEWATER SOUTHERN was a 1,200-volt interurban linking Stockton with Modesto. The 34-mile line began electric operation in 1913 and soon was acquired by the Western Pacific. It had only three interurban cars, two of which, above, were awaiting passengers in Modesto about 1915. The Tidewater borrowed trailers from the Central California Traction on the rare occasions when business boomed. The line had two electric locomotives but occasionally leased the Oakland, Antioch & Eastern 101 (Sacramento Northern 601) when business was brisk. Passenger service ceased in 1932 but there was electric freight operation until 1948. The road also had a non-electrified branch to Turlock and an electrified line to Manteca.

Ted Wurm Collection

THE VISALIA ELECTRIC adopted the unusual 3,300-volt, 15-cycle alternating current system in 1908 when it commenced electrified service over portions of Southern Pacific and its own track. The SP, which controlled the VE, used the interurban in Tulare County's citrus area as a testing ground for AC, while studies were conducted for mainline electrification that never occurred. Box cab motor 601, above, hauled freight under the high-voltage wires from 1908 until the end of electrification in 1944. Arch-windowed 101, below, built by American in 1907, lasted until electric passenger service ceased in 1924. Trailers acquired on the same order were sent to the Pacific Electric during World War I, and two steel cars ended up on the Napa Valley also after service on the Pacific Electric.

Above, Ted Wurm Collection;
below, Vernon J. Sappers Collection

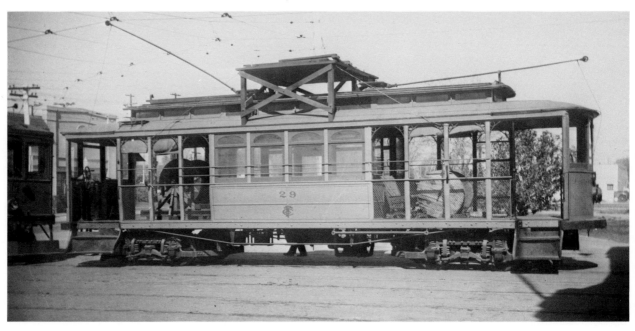

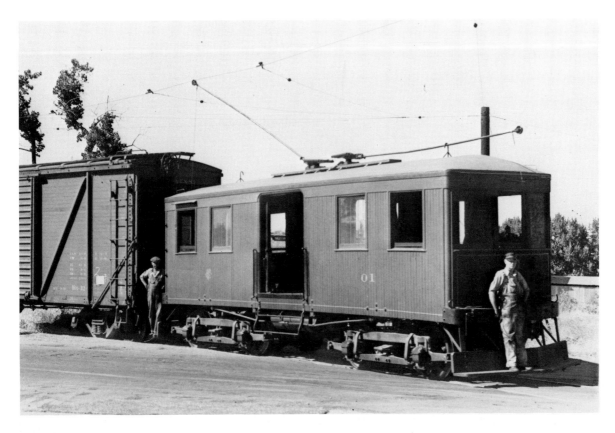

FRESNO TRACTION was controlled by Los Angeles streetcar magnate Henry Huntington from 1903 until Southern Pacific gained control in 1910. Early in this century, three cars and 25 employees of predecessor Fresno City Railway posed by the carbarn. Note the polished brass uniform buttons. Line car 29, below, was delivered as a passenger car in 1909 by American Car Company. On this page, freight motor 01, built in 1903 by Brill, switched a freight spur in the late 1930s. Below, Birney 74 was running at F and Los Angeles streets in 1938, a year before service was discontinued. Another road, the Fresno Interurban, operated electrically from 1916-18.

Opposite, above, Pacific Gas and Electric Co.;
below, Ted Wurm; above, Charles A. Smallwood;
below, Marvin Maynard

BAKERSFIELD & KERN Electric operated a variety of cars in the hub of the southern San Joaquin Valley, which prospered both from agriculture and petroleum. Shortly before abandonment on February 28, 1942, Birney 20, above, loaded at the Santa Fe depot. The car originally ran in Santa Cruz and later was sold to Halifax, Nova Scotia. Either the 8 or 9 is shown below in the 1920s and, on the page opposite, are two of the 10-15 class built by American Car Company in 1911. The 13, above, was retained until the end for school service. The other car, photographed about 1920, has shades drawn in the open section to protect passengers from inclement weather.

Bottom, both pages, R. T. Hill;
above, opposite, Ted Wurm Collection;
above, George Henderson

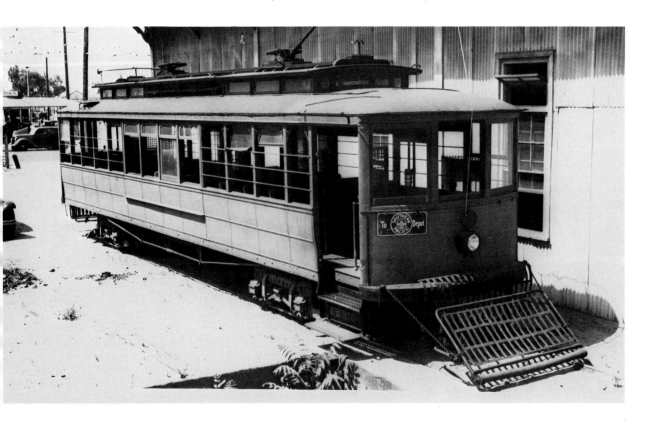

Traction
Along the
Central
Coast

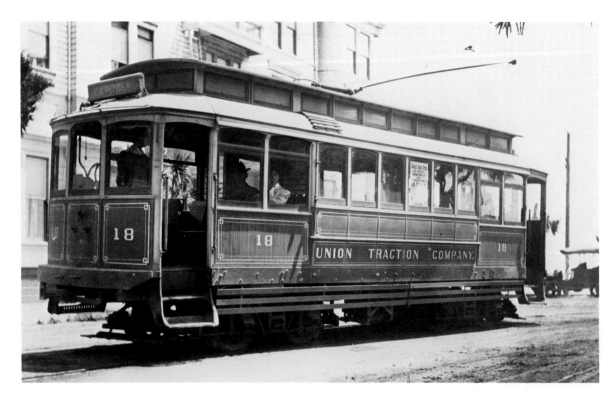

THE ELECTRIC RAILWAY developed early in the seaside cities of Santa Cruz and Monterey and was abandoned before most systems were in California. Santa Cruz became the Coney Island or Atlantic City of San Francisco and offered a death-defying roller coaster and thrill-filled boardwalk and dancing pavilion along the Pacific Ocean. Monterey, the old Spanish and Mexican capital of Alta California, developed into a fish canning center immortalized by John Steinbeck in *Cannery Row*. Its posh Del Monte Hotel and Pacific Grove suburb to the south became havens for the very wealthy, especially after Southern Pacific inaugurated the elegant *Del Monte* from San

Francisco in 1889. On the page opposite are two views of the Santa Cruz system, known during most of its history as Union Traction Company. The cars ran along the beach past the boardwalk and casino, above, and the sprawling Sea Beach Hotel, below, which burned in 1912. Santa Cruz 18, above, an early product of St. Louis Car Company, was awaiting passengers in Capitola in 1920. In the scene below, the car that shuttled over a short spur to the Casa Del Rey Hotel in Santa Cruz shares the street with two horseless carriages, also in 1920.

Opposite, Charles A. Smallwood Collection;
this page, R. T. Hill

THE ORIGIN of Union Traction's open cars has baffled historians, but the car rolling on Pacific Avenue in 1920 has the look of a J.G. Brill product and would not seem out of place in New England where this type of car was common. The 19, center, was built by the pioneering Carter Brothers factory in Newark, north of San Jose, and one source states it had rare Walker traction motors. The 14, below, was running in Seabright service early in the century. *Below, Randolph Brandt Collection; others, R. T. Hill, Vernon J. Sappers Collection*

THE HEYDAY and the end of Santa Cruz streetcars is shown in these two views. A crowd boarding a Capitola-bound car in 1912 shows how popular and essential street railways were before there were automobiles and good roads. "The Best Place To Eat" coffee shop offered a "Free Reading Room" on the right. Santa Cruz cars usually promoted seaside activities such as the dance advertised on the dash sign. Below, the Birney car had met its match in 1924 and the future seemed obvious when Mayor John Maher posed with the car and a shiny new bus. Union Traction abandoned streetcars in January 1926. Birney 23 was sold to Bakersfield which resold the car to Halifax, Nova Scotia. *Charles A. Smallwood Collection*

A HORSECAR LINE built between Monterey and Pacific Grove was the beginnings of the Monterey & Pacific Grove Railway, which inaugurated electric service between its namesake cities in 1903. At first narrow-gauged horsecar rails were used, but the system was converted to standard gauge in 1905. Initially, the cars had Monterey's streets pretty much to themselves, above, but by the 1920s, below, motor vehicles were competing for space on Alvarado Street. The M&PG was one of the first streetcar systems to be abandoned in California. Service ceased in July 1923.

Above, Charles A. Smallwood Collection; below, R. T. Hill

SOME OF THE original cars acquired in 1904 from St. Louis Car Company lasted until abandonment. One of Monterey's 5-7 type was rolling over a dusty street, above, shortly before the cars quit in 1923. One of the more obscure California electric railways is shown below. Watsonville Transportation Company began service in 1904 with two of these cars running on three-foot-gauge track between Watsonville and a wharf. The line connected with the steam-operated (and also three-foot-gauge) Pajaro Valley Consolidated Railroad. The electric line went bankrupt in 1905 and was reorganized in 1911, after being left idle for more than five years. Service resumed but the company was unable to repair the pier after storm damage, so management abandoned the railroad in 1913.

Above, R. T. Hill; below, Ted Wurm Collection

Traction In Southern California

SOUTHERN CALIFORNIA was truly the hub of electric railway development west of Chicago. Few areas in the United States could match the Southland for variety and size of streetcar and interurban systems. In the heyday of electric traction, more than 2,000 streetcars and interurbans were operated daily by the two principal Los Angeles companies, Pacific Electric and Los Angeles Railway. The PE was one of the nation's largest originators of freight traffic and dispatched 2,700 passenger trains a day over 1,000 miles of track. Perhaps no two symbols were more illustrative of Los Angeles during their respective eras than, above, the "Huntington Standard" streetcar, representing the early years of the City of Angels, and the City Hall, which pointed toward the future when there would be no streetcars. The photo was taken in 1940 on the Los Angeles Railway's narrow-gauged streetcar loop on the grounds of the new Los Angeles Union Passenger Depot. On the page opposite are two eras of the vast PE system. Above, in the late 1930s, a big red 1100-type car on the Pasadena Short Line is about to swing off Main Street into the bustling Sixth and Main Streets station. The end of the "World's Largest Interurban" is only about a year away in the bottom photo, taken of an approaching Los Angeles-bound car that had originally been built for Southern Pacific's Oakland suburban electric operation. The last PE rail line was abandoned in April 1961.

Below, Harre W. Demoro; others, Waldemar Sievers

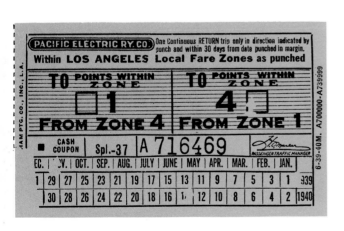

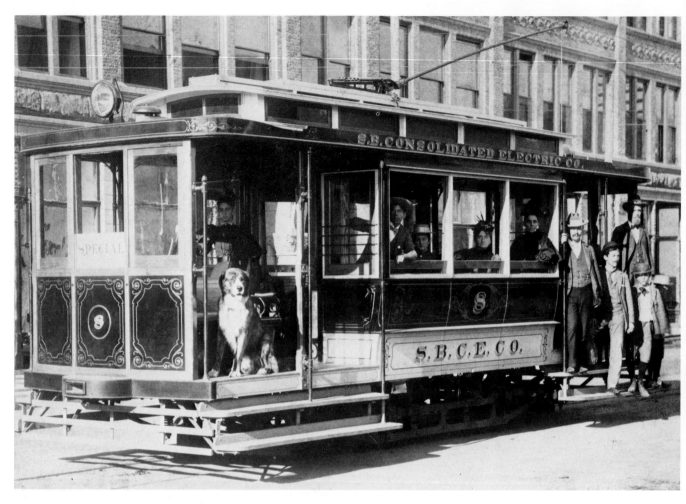

SANTA BARBARA had one of Southern California's smaller streetcar systems, which was owned for a time by Southern California Edison Company. The road was one of the first city systems to be abandoned; the last car ran in the early hours of July 1, 1929. One of Santa Barbara's early California type cars, shown on the page opposite, with traction mascot Towser staring at the camera, was built in 1896 by San Francisco manufacturer Hammond, and retired in 1913. One of two modern double-truck, center-door cars built in 1913 by Brill, is shown opposite, below. Above is a Birney car acquired secondhand from San Diego in 1924. Perhaps the state's most obscure electric line, the three-foot-gauge Pacific Coast Railway, operated one car in the San Luis Obispo area: the steel center-door interurban shown below.

Opposite, top, Ted Wurm Collection;
below, Marvin T. Maynard; others, R. T. Hill

From The Mountains To The Sea

WHAT WAS TO BECOME the World's Largest Interurban was still a gaggle of small traction systems in 1905 when, above, a Fourth of July crowd arrived at Santa Monica for an outing on the Pacific shore. The cars belong to the Los Angeles Pacific, which was merged into Pacific Electric in 1911. On the page opposite, top, an early Los Angeles-Long Beach car loads in a dirt street, perhaps on July 4, 1902, opening day for the route, which would survive as PE's last line until April 8, 1961. Starting in 1907 PE rebuilt these cars with stronger bodies and more powerful motors and the 219, renumbered 519, was not retired until 1934. One of the most spectacular railroad journeys in the world was PE's line up Mount Lowe where, opposite bottom, cars lurched around the Circular Bridge and gave patrons the sensation of flight.   *Above, Terry Wilkerson collection; opposite, Ira L. Swett collection*

THE HUNTINGTON BUILDING, opened in 1905 at Sixth and Main streets, was the first tall office building in a city worried about earthquakes. The building, shown opposite top shortly after completion, housed PE (and later Southern Pacific) offices and was the principal center city interurban station. At the rear of the building, below opposite, were both surface tracks and an elevated terminal. In this view taken in 1940, the 995 on the left is assigned to the once-a-day Santa Monica Air Line and the 1212, right, is awaiting a call for service to San Bernardino. The elevated trainsheds are directly above the cars. On this page, the end of PE service was near when a former Southern Pacific-Oakland car on the elevated tracks awaited Long Beach traffic on a warm December 1959 evening. Below, the elevated ramp ended at Ninth Street and a former Portland, Oregon, car is ascending toward the Huntington Building after a fast run from Santa Ana in 1940. *Opposite, top, Ira L. Swett Magna collection; this page, top, Harre W. Demoro; others, Waldemar Sievers*

WOODEN CARS were standard on the Pacific Electric until the tragic Vineyard wreck in 1913 when the company shifted engineering to steel designs. The last big order of wooden equipment was for 45 cars (plus eight for the Peninsular Railway) from Jewett in 1913. The five-window front that was a characteristic of Los Angeles traction design is evident, left, in the view in 1950 at Ocean Park near Santa Monica. Prior to World War II, even big PE cars were required by Los Angeles ordinance to have basket-like streetcar fenders. Fender-equipped PE 1008, below, is en route to Alhambra and the San Gabriel Mission as it passes Los Angeles Union Passenger Station in 1940, a year before buses replaced the cars. Another major wooden car series was 950-993, top, page opposite, which were built by St. Louis Car Company in 1907 for the Los Angeles Pacific. They are shown here in their original 700 number series on the Pasadena Short Line about 1920. The 1422, below, was built in 1909 by St. Louis Car Company as interurban 544 and has air-operated pole trolleys, used widely on PE and briefly on the Northern Electric. The car became passenger-baggage car 1304 in 1935, then box motor 1422 when it was assigned as a switch engine at the Macy Street Shops in 1940, where it served until 1951.

Left, Fred H. Matthews Jr. — BAERA;
top opposite, Roy E. Healy collection — BAERA;
others, Waldemar Sievers

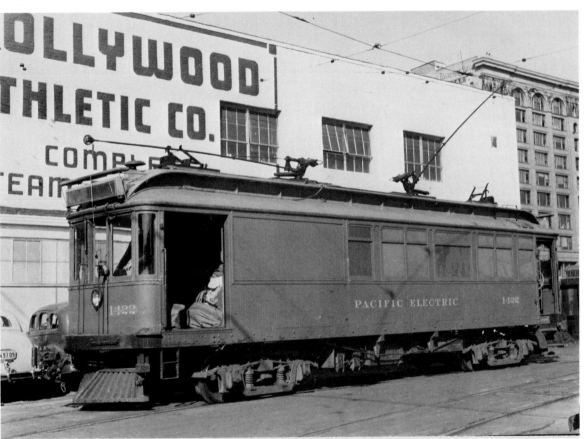

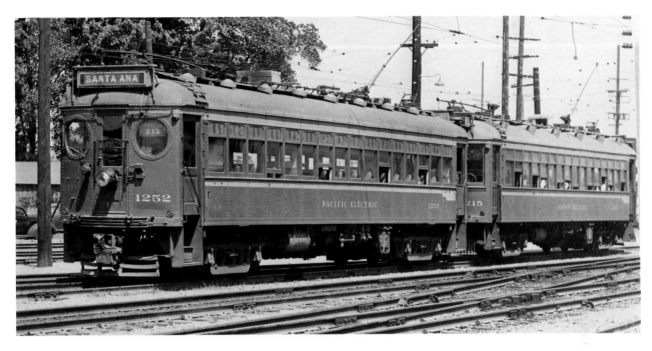

PE'S PREMIER INTERURBAN CARS were in the 1200 series and comprised four distinct groups. On the page opposite, car 1237 was a "Long Beach Twelve" built in 1921 by Pullman and shown in 1934 in its namesake city. The original series, 1200-1221, arrived from Pressed Steel in 1915 for the San Bernardino line. This class originally had lavatories, but they had been removed by the time San Pedro-bound 1209, opposite below, rolled into Watts over the four-track main line in 1945. A local car is loading on the outside track for Los Angeles. Said to be the fastest in the series were 1252-1263, above, built in 1912 by Pullman and acquired secondhand from SP's Oregon lines in 1928. The final 1200 was the elegant 1299, shown below on the four-tracked Huntington Drive route to Pasadena and passing a Sierra Vista local in 1951. It was rebuilt from an Oregon car for company officials and also used on the deluxe "Commodore" service to Newport Beach until 1949.

Opposite top, J. Allen Hawkins; below, Waldemar Sievers; this page, top, Bill Johns; below, Fred H. Matthews Jr. — BAERA

PE'S LAST INTERURBANS were hand-me-downs from two SP-owned systems in the San Francisco Bay Area that were abandoned in 1941. Long Beach-bound 409, above, whistling past a local car at the Watts carhouse in 1957, was one of about 70 former Interurban Electric (Oakland, Alameda and Berkeley lines) cars that went to PE during World War II. The 300, shown below arriving in 1957 at Sixth and Main station from Bellflower, was among 19 former Northwestern Pacific cars that had run in Marin County. The ex-Bay Area cars closed out PE service in 1961. *Both, Harre W. Demoro*

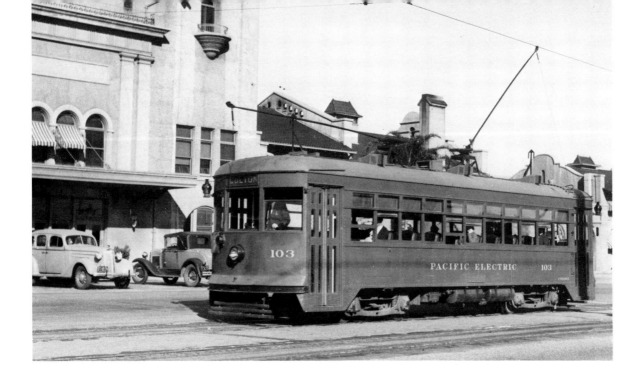

DOZENS OF DIFFERENT KINDS of wooden and steel cars were used by PE in local service, including Hedley-Doyle "Stepless" type, Birneys, PCC cars, wooden equipment and open cars. Car 103, above, at San Bernardino in 1937, was built by St. Louis Car Company in 1930 and sold to Vera Cruz, Mexico, in 1950, where it ran for many more years. Car 152, below in 1938 at Colton, is an ex-Fresno Traction "Double Truck Birney"

built by St. Louis Car Company in 1925. For other views of these much-traveled Fresno cars, see pages on Fresno, Central California Traction Co. and Sacramento. PE had three of the cars and ran them until 1941. Note how PE blocked off doors when the cars were converted to one-man operation.

Above, Waldemar Sievers; below, Vernon J. Sappers

PE'S "HOLLYWOOD CARS" began as 160 plain-appearing city cars built in 1922, 1923 and 1928 by St. Louis Car Company and in 1925 by Brill. The 623 in its original condition speeds along the Sierra Vista line in 1935 while, below, a modernized and speeded-up 697 exits one of the tunnels on Hill Street in 1940. At the bottom of the page, the cars have been converted to one-man operation and are numbered in the 5050 series. The scene, bottom, at Beverly Hills on September 25, 1954, is a sad one, for buses will replace the railcars the following day.

Bottom, Harre W. Demoro; others, Waldemar Sievers

LINES TO THE WEST began using a downtown subway and station in 1925. "Hollywood Type" 5131 was awaiting passengers for its namesake destination in the early hours of September 26, 1954, about an hour before the rail line was replaced by buses. Below, PE's often-called "Dream Right of Way" in the Hollywood Freeway median through Cahuenga Pass was used until 1952 by lines to the San Fernando Valley. Two 5050-type cars en route to Los Angeles were photographed near Mulholland Drive in 1950.

Above, Harre W. Demoro; below, Waldemar Sievers

FREIGHT TRAFFIC, not passengers, was the lifeblood of Pacific Electric which quickly became a major freight feeder to parent Southern Pacific. Box motor traffic using single cars carrying express and freight and sometimes mail were common in PE's heyday. On the page opposite, top, the cars await loads at the produce market between Seventh and Eighth Streets. Many cars also converged at the Los Angeles Union Passenger Station, below opposite, where express from mainline trains was handled. There was so much traffic during World War II that, above, PE rebuilt this surplus Oregon interurban car into a railway post office car, and didn't take time to remove the window posts. Below, PE also had a larger fleet of electric locomotives for cars interchanged with the steam roads. This scene was taken at 92nd Street near Watts in 1947.

Opposite, top, Ira L. Swett Magna collection;
others, Waldemar Sievers

Huntington's
Yellow Cars

WHEN THE TRACTION TITANS fought their last battle in Los Angeles in 1911, the Southern Pacific interests led by E.H. Harriman consolidated the standard-gauged properties into the Pacific Electric, and Henry Huntington was left with the 42-inch-gauge Los Angeles Railway local system, which for many years was the largest electric railway in the West — with close to 1,500 cars at its peak. One of the system's classic car styles was the ungainly appearing "Sowbelly," shown above with the city in the background as it coasts down the Fifth Street hill toward Figueroa Street in 1947, shortly before the center-entrance cars were retired. LARY's first double-truck steel cars were the H Type, shown opposite, top, in 1940 on the Union Station loop. The 1209 was in the first group of H types delivered by St. Louis Car Company in 1921, and it originally had couplers for train operation. One of the narrow-gauged system's 70 Birney Safety Cars is depicted below. These were the first cars bought "off the shelf" instead of being built to LARY designs, and they were not particularly successful, although a few ran as late as 1946.

Above, Bill Johns-Ira L. Swett Standard collection;
others, Waldemar Sievers

HIGH STEPS made streetcars slow loading and were unpopular with the public, especially with women who wore long skirts, so Los Angeles Railway embarked on a major modernization program which resulted in the reconstruction of 107 old cars and 76 new ones built by the St. Louis Car Company which thought enough of the low-step, drop-center design to display one of the cars at the Panama-Pacific International Exposition in San Francisco in 1915. The cars could not be converted to one-man operation and the last Sowbellies ran in 1947.

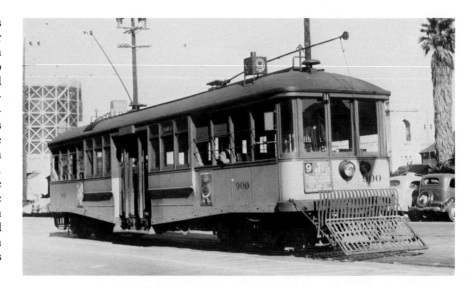

THE "STANDARD" Los Angeles streetcar both on LARY and Pacific Electric in the early history of Southland traction was the "Huntington Standard" shown above near Los Angeles Union Passenger Terminal in 1940. LARY owned about 800 and some ran as late as 1952. The 1160, right, in post-World War II Los Angeles Transit Lines colors, was rebuilt from a short "Huntington Standard" in the early 1920s. Note the high step.

Right, Ira L. Swett-Standard
collection;
others Waldemar Sievers

TYPE H 1293 had been repainted in Los Angeles Transit Lines yellow, green and white but still had its massive Eclipse fender in 1947 as it rolled through the Civic Center on the 7 line that ran south from downtown to 116th Street and South Broadway. The vintage 1923 car had been rebuilt with folding doors and had lost its coupler for train operation, which was discontinued in 1930. To soothe the public after it received a fare increase, LARY remodeled 35 H type cars in the late 1920s, installing leather-upholstered seats and improved lighting. Exteriors were given flashy green paint, which set the cars apart from their less elegant contemporaries in traditional yellow. Had the Great Depression not intervened, more probably would have been converted.

Above, Waldemar Sievers; below, Interurban Press

CURBSIDE PARKING already was at a premium on Broadway south of Third Street in 1929, but LARY streetcars passing the massive old City Hall, right, had the center of the street to themselves. Although the outside world still saw Los Angeles as a balmy semi-tropical vacationland with glittering Hollywood movie stars—and little else—the City of Angels was well on its way to becoming California's largest metropolitan area. Soon, Wall Street would crash and the Los Angeles Basin would be the beacon for hundreds of thousands of refugees from the Dust Bowl and other unfortunate locales. The spectacular growth would bring more automobiles but not more streetcar riders.   *Security-First National Bank*

NEW TRACK WAS being laid at West Fifth and South Olive Streets in 1945 as an old "Standard" on the right met a glistening new PCC Car on the left. In the view below, a pair of "Standards" speed along the wide private right-of-way on South Vermont Avenue on the F line. The broad median was necessary because, until it was merged into the Pacific Electric and rerouted and changed to standard gauge, the narrow-gauged Los Angeles & Redondo interurban line also had a track here.

Above, Waldemar Sievers;
below, Ira L. Swett-Standard collection

THE V LINE, a major crosstown route that had Type H and PCC cars, survived until the abandonment of the narrow-gauged system in 1963. Type H 1326, page opposite, at Vernon and Santa Fe in 1952, had been "modernized" with skirting, folding doors and modern fenders, but still had the two open sections, which were ideal for warm Southern California days. The LATL motorman on the 7 line has Johnson farebox, money changer and captain's seat. The air brake gauge is on the post to his right. One of LARY's longest lines ran to Inglewood and Hawthorne. In this World War II scene, above, the Hawthorne-bound car carries an advertisement for an article on "Germany's Evil Genius." Left, traffic was so busy at Spring and Main streets that PE and LARY movements were controlled by this elevated tower. *Opposite, top, Ira L. Swett-Standard collection; below, Norman K. Johnson; above, Waldemar Sievers; below, Raymond E. Younghans*

LOS ANGELES was one of the first cities to have sleek new PCC cars, which were based on industry-sponsored research in the early 1930s. The first Los Angeles Railway PCC, left, was posed for publicity purposes shortly after it arrived in 1937. One of the 1937 cars, built by St. Louis Car Company, paused below on private right-of-way on the R line about 1950. It had been repainted in the National City Lines green, white and yellow. On the page opposite, all three styles of LARY PCCs pose in Metropolitan Transportation Authority green in 1963 at Division 20 shortly before the system was abandoned. The second and third cars from the left were acquired in 1943-44, the car second from right arrived in 1948. The crowd scene was taken in March 1937 when the PCCs were introduced by actress Shirley Temple. On the page opposite, bottom, is one of the PCCs built in 1948 by St. Louis Car Company.

Left, Ira L. Swett-Magna collection; below, Robert Coon; opposite, top, Richard Smith; center, E. MacDonald Leo; below, Addison H. Laflin Jr. — BAERA

PCC CAR 3009 was almost identical to the first PCCs built for Brooklyn, San Diego and Baltimore, but had narrow-gauged 42-inch-gauge trucks. The 3009 was built in 1937 and still was in service in 1963 when the lines were abandoned. "Standard" 436 in yellow LARY colors in 1940 laid over at Lincoln Park, below, which had an entry arch worthy of a temple or a Hollywood set. On this page, a Sowbelly operates over dual-gauged trackage between the two Hill Street tunnels in 1940. There are three rails so PE and LARY cars can share the trackage. Note the 10-cent parking rate for two hours. In the center view, two "Standards" on the F and U lines meet on Vermont Avenue at Florence Avenue in 1945. The Sowbelly in the bottom view is on West Adams Boulevard near Orange Drive in 1945. The A line ran into West Los Angeles.

This page and opposite, top, Waldemar Sievers; center, opposite, Alfred Haij; below, Chard Walker

The Other Streetcar In Glendale

WHEN THE GLENDALE & Montrose Railway began as the narrow-gauged Glendale & Eagle Rock in 1909 it was such a small operation it lacked a carbarn and stored rolling stock on the street overnight. The line was sold to a cement company in 1916 which extended the operation and completed the road's conversion to standard gauge in 1917. The road never got much beyond Glendale and never reached central Los Angeles; instead, it depended on the Los Angeles Railway and Pacific Electric Railway for outside connections. The first cars, such as the narrow-gauged one-spot above, were acquired secondhand from LARY. On the page opposite is the brawny Baldwin-Westinghouse electric motor acquired new in 1923 as part of an arrangement with the Union Pacific. G&M 22 eventually passed to UP's Yakima Valley Transportation Company in Washington state, where, below, it operated until 1985.

Both pages, Craig Rasmussen Collection

GLENDALE & MONTROSE and Pacific Electric both built lines on East Broadway in Glendale. After PE tore its line up in 1906, G&M laid narrow-gauge rails. The view, above, was taken in 1910 at the Brand Boulevard terminal, where connections were made by Glendale & Eagle Rock cars with PE's interurban line to Los Angeles. In 1914, PE and G&M jointly built a standard-gauged line on Broadway. While the photos on the page opposite are not of the highest quality, they are among the few views that have survived of G&M's three double-trucked Birney cars built in 1923 by American Car Company. After abandonment of passenger service in 1930, the three cars, finest to run on G&M, were stored at PE's Torrance Shops. The 10, above, and 12, below, apparently were given to San Diego Electric Railway in 1937 which operated them until 1947, but car 11 was scrapped by PE in 1940. An ex-G&M car in San Diego is shown on page 196.   *Both pages, Craig Rasmussen Collection*

Traction Along San Diego Bay

SAN DIEGO wasn't much of a place until the Spreckels family decided to make it a real city by sponsoring great public works, including the consolidation of various traction systems and interurban lines into the San Diego Electric Railway. While hardly the largest streetcar system on the coast, the SDERy was one of the best managed and had some of the best rolling stock. Perhaps the zenith of San Diego streetcar design was reached in 1923 when the Spreckels put 50 lightweight cars (numbered in the 400 series) in service as part of a modernization that included a new line to La Jolla. Above, this page, one of the 400s heads downtown from Balboa Park, site of two expositions and to become the location of a world-famous zoo. Above, opposite, is a center-door car built for the exposition at Balboa Park in 1915. The 147, below, was built in 1912 by St. Louis Car Company and was kept for emergency service during World War II when thousands of servicemen and war workers mobbed San Diego.

Above, Fred H. Matthews, Jr. — BAERA;
others, Addison H. Laflin Jr. — BAERA

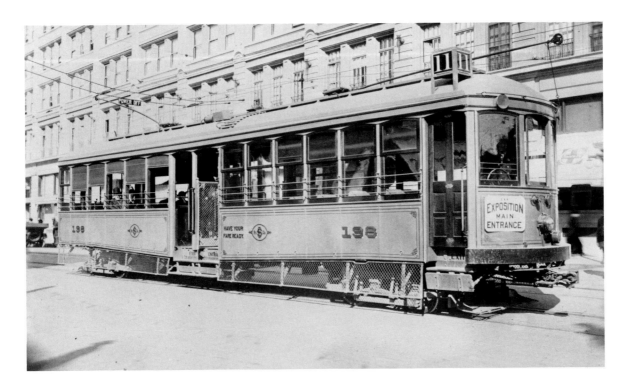

COORDINATED rail-truck express service was tried briefly in the 1920s to Mission Beach. The seaside beauty and climate at Coronado made it a vacation destination. Before the turn of the century the tourists rode the little cars, center, of the Coronado Railroad. The motorman is changing trolley poles at the line's Coronado Hotel terminal in the 1890s. Below is a two-car train of the 400-series cars built by American in 1923-24 for the splendid new La Jolla interurban. The La Jolla line was abandoned in 1940 but the 400s ran until the streetcar system was replaced by buses in 1949.

Below, Lorin Silleman—BAERA;
others, BAERA archives

SECONDHAND cars were obtained from three cities to help shoulder the war effort: Above, a creaky but dependable ex-Third Avenue Railway car, built in 1905 by Brill, now far from the streets of Gotham, and running its last miles in sunny San Diego; right, an ex-Wilkes-Barre, Pennsylvania, car built by American Car Company in 1922; below, a former Salt Lake City car built in 1927 also by American.

Three photos,
Addison H. Laflin Jr. — BAERA

THE HIGH BRIDGE at Balboa Park was one of the most photographed scenes in San Diego streetcar history. When this photo was taken in 1947, the Spreckels still owned the company but soon would sell it to bus promoter Jesse L. Haugh, who abandoned the rail system in 1949. The car below was bought secondhand from the Glendale & Montrose for Coronado service.

Above, Fred H. Matthews Jr. — BAERA;
below, Addison H. Laflin Jr. — BAERA

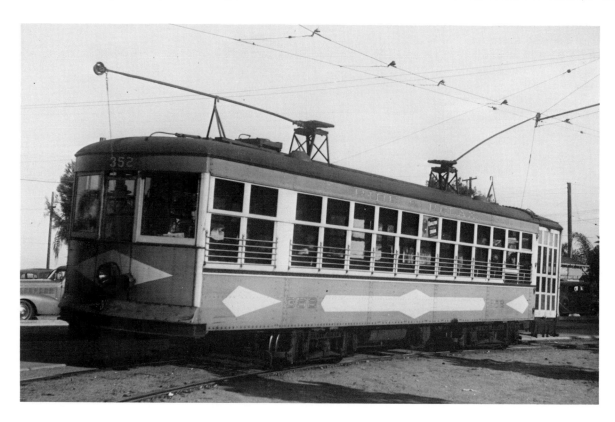

SAN DIEGO WAS one of the first cities to buy PCC cars, acquiring 25 of the rubber-cushioned, smooth-riding cars from St. Louis Car Company in 1937 and three more in 1938. The whisper-quiet cars triggered spectacular gains in ridership and performed extremely well on San Diego's well-maintained track.

They were still in excellent condition when rail service was abandoned in 1949 and most found new careers on the El Paso-Juarez international streetcar line where they ran into the 1970s. *Both, Addison H. Laflin Jr. — BAERA*

THE ELECTRIC RAILWAY returned to San Diego in 1981 with the opening of a new light rail line using German-built cars between downtown and the U.S.-Mexico border. Much of the line was built on the San Diego & Arizona Railroad. Right, a three-car train bound for the border stops under the high-voltage lines at 24th Street in National City. Below, a two-car train at H Street in Chula Vista. Opposite, the interior of one of the spacious cars and, below, the downtown terminal in the street at the Santa Fe (Amtrak) passenger train station. A second line opened in 1986. *Both pages, Harre W. Demoro*

THE FILLMORE HILL counterbalance was a spectacular street-car ride using two cars linked by an underground cable to prevent runaways on the steep grade. In this remarkable photograph taken in the mid-1930s, the two cars pass at Fillmore and Vallejo streets against a background of San Francisco Bay and Angel Island. A Southern Pacific Golden Gate Ferries Ltd. diesel-electric is en route to Sausalito from the Hyde Street Pier.   *Waldemar Sievers*

California Traction Lines

THIS LIST IS BASED on the *McGraw Electric Railway Directory* for 1931, published 1931 by McGraw-Hill Catalog and Directory Co., New York. The number after the city name is the city's population at that time. All listings are 550-600 volts DC, standard gauge, overhead trolley, unless otherwise noted.

BAKERSFIELD (26,015)
Bakersfield & Kern Electric Ry. Co., 11 motor cars, 1 service car, 10.18 track miles; fares 10 cents, 7 for $1 tokens, $1 weekly pass.

EXETER (2,685)
Visalia Electric Railroad, 3 motor cars, 2 service cars, 2 locomotives, track miles, 68.48. (This data apparently is outdated as passenger service has been abandoned and one of the locomotives listed is probably a gas-electric.) Voltage, 3,300 AC, 15 cycles.

EUREKA (15,752)
Eureka Street Railway, 15 motor cars, 1 service, 12 track miles; 1 motor bus.

FRESNO (52,513)
Fresno Traction Co., 46 motor cars, 1 freight motor, 2 service cars, 48.67 track miles; fares, 7 cents, 3 tokens for 20 cents.

LOS ANGELES (1,238,048)
Los Angeles Motor Coach Co., 74 buses, 50.75 route miles; fares, 6 and 10 cents. (Owned by PE and LARY.)

Los Angeles Railway Corp., motor cars, 1,226, 11 freight motor, service cars 116, track miles 403.7, gauge, 42"; fares, 7 cents, four tokens for 25 cents. Motor buses, 105 on 95.61 route miles.

Pacific Electric Railway Co., 804 passenger cars (motor 777, trail 27), 2,355 freight cars (of which 36 were motorized), 113 service cars, 53 locomotives, voltages 600 and 1,200 DC. Motor buses, 141 on 207.18 route miles.

NAPA (6,437)
San Francisco, Napa & Calistoga Railway, 14 passenger cars (9 motor, 5 trail), 20 freight cars (2 motor, 18 trail), 5 service cars, 1 electric locomotive, 48.54 track miles, voltage 3,300 AC, 25 cycles; 2 buses operated by subsidiary Napa Valley Bus Co. on 41.60 route miles.

OAKLAND (284,063)
Castro Point Railway & Terminal Co., at Richmond, Calif., operated by Key System and others over 2.2 miles. Affiliated with Blake quarry operation.

Railway Equipment & Realty Co. Ltd. controls Key System Ltd., Key Terminal Railway Ltd., East Bay Street Railways Ltd., and East Bay Motor Coach Lines Ltd. Grand total: 473 motor passenger cars (trailers not shown), 16 freight (8 motor, 8 trail), 52 service, 3 electric locomotives, 67 buses, 4 ferries. (Note, from 1939 to 1958, Key System transbay trains used overrunning third rail on the San Francisco-Oakland Bay Bridge and approaches.)

East Bay Motor Coach Lines Ltd., 37.42 route miles; fare 7 cents.

East Bay Street Railways Ltd., 180.59 track miles; fare 7 cents.

Key System Ltd., 56.62 track miles; fares, 21 cents, monthly commute, $6.50.

Key Terminal Railway Ltd., 9.39 track miles, fares same as Key System Ltd.

PETALUMA (8,245)
Petaluma & Santa Rosa Railroad, 9 motor cars, 89 freight (trail) cars, 5 service cars, 6 locomotives, track miles 49.78.

SACRAMENTO (93,750)
Pacific Gas and Electric Co., Sacramento Street Railway Division, 75 motor cars, 2 service, 46.59 track miles; fares 7 cents, 4 tokens for 25 cents, $1.50 weekly pass; 11 motor buses on 10.77 route miles.

Sacramento Northern Railway, 82 passenger cars (54 motor, 28 trail), 311 freight (trail), 66 service, 25 electric locomotives, 353.57 track miles, voltage, 600-1,200-1,500 DC; fares, 3.61 cents and 5 cents per mile; buses, 1 on 25 route miles. Some lines had 600-volt overrunning third rail.

SAN DIEGO (147,995)
San Diego Electric Railway Co., 147 motor cars, 31 freight (trail), 22 service, 1 electric locomotive, 95.21 track miles; fares, zones, 5 cents, tokens 4 for 30 cents, also tickets; 85 buses on 78.89 route miles.

SAN FRANCISCO (634,394)
Market Street Railway Co., 771 (including 725 motor and 46 trail, which were cable cars), 58 service, 281.96 track miles; fares, 5 cents; 6 buses on 8.93 route miles.

Municipal Railway of San Francisco, 234 motor cars, 6 service, 1 locomotive, 78.11 track miles; fare, 7 cents; motor buses, 18 on 10.96 route miles.

Southern Pacific, East Bay Electric Division, 147 cars (87 motor, 60 trail), 3 locomotives, track miles 118.84. Voltage, 1,200 DC. (Note: The locomotives were not on the property and had been leased to other SP subsidiaries.)

SAN JOSE (57,651)

Peninsular Railway Co., 34 motor cars, 5 freight (1 motor, 4 trail), 6 service, 91.11 track miles; fares 6 cents to 85 cents, tokens 4 for 25 cents; buses, 11 on 8.41 route miles, fares 6 and 10 cents.

San Jose Railroads, 44 cars (41 motor, 3 trail), 45.22 track miles; fares, 10 cents, 4 tokens for 25 cents; buses, 1 on 3.13 route miles.

SAN LUIS OBISPO (8,276)

Pacific Coast Railway Co., 1 motor car, 3 electric locomotives, 11.32 track miles, gauge, 3 feet.

SAUSALITO (3,500)

Northwestern Pacific Railroad Co., 66 cars (44 motor, 22 trail), 1 service, 40.40 track miles; all lines overrunning third rail.

SOUTH SAN FRANCISCO (6,193)

South San Francisco Railroad & Power Co., controlled by Market Street Railway Co., 4 motor cars, 3.16 track miles; fare, 5 cents.

STOCKTON (47,963)

Central California Traction Co., 17 cars (15 motor, 2 trail), 1 service, 4 electric locomotives, 77.91 track miles. Voltage, 1,200 volts DC, with underrunning third rail outside cities.

Stockton Electric Railroad Co., 40 passenger cars, 2 service, 28.37 track miles; fares, 7 cents, 4 tokens for 25 cents; buses, 2 on 1.6 route miles, fares 7 cents, 6¼ cent tokens.

Tidewater Southern Railway Co., 3 motor cars, 4 service, 2 electric locomotives, 85 track miles. Voltage 1,200 DC.

Note: The Glendale & Montrose just missed the list, being abandoned on December 30, 1930.

Several systems owned ferries and other floating equipment. SP, assigned ferries from its San Francisco Bay operations; Key System in 1931 had four ferries which replaced six older craft; Northwestern Pacific's fleet varied in size but had 3 ferries in 1931; Sacramento Northern had a distillate gasoline-powered ferry that took entire trains across the San Joaquin-Sacramento River delta; Petaluma & Santa Rosa owned sternwheeled riverboats.

Saved Cars

MUNICIPAL RAILWAY OF SAN FRANCISCO RETAINED BY CITY FOR SUMMER FESTIVAL

Municipal Railway of San Francisco 1, streetcar
Municipal Railway of San Francisco 130, streetcar
Market Street Railway 578, streetcar
Municipal Railway of San Francisco 1006, PCC Car
Municipal Railway of San Francisco 1040, PCC Car
Municipal Railway of San Francisco 1128, PCC Car
Market Street Railway 798, streetcar (b)
(A number of PCC cars are in dead storage)

ORANGE EMPIRE RAILWAY MUSEUM PERRIS

Bakersfield & Kern 4, streetcar
Fresno Traction 51, Hedley-Doyle (b)

Fresno Traction 83, streetcar (b)
Glendale & Montrose 22, freight motor
Key System 167, articulated unit
Los Angeles Railway 7, streetcar
Los Angeles Railway 152, streetcar
Los Angeles Railway 525, streetcar
Los Angeles Railway 665, streetcar
Los Angeles Railway 936, "Sowbelly" (b)
Los Angeles Railway 1069, Birney (b)
Los Angeles Railway 1160, streetcar
Los Angeles Railway 1201, streetcar
Los Angeles Railway 1423, streetcar
Los Angeles Railway 1450, streetcar
Los Angeles Railway 1559, streetcar
Los Angeles Railway 2501, streetcar (b)
Los Angeles Railway 2601, streetcar
Los Angeles Railway 3001, PCC Car
Los Angeles Railway 3100, PCC Car
Los Angeles Transit Lines 3165, PCC Car

Los Angeles Railway "Descanso," funeral car
Los Angeles Railway 9209, power car
Los Angeles Railway 9225, derrick
Los Angeles Railway 9310, rail grinder
Los Angeles Railway 9350, line car
Los Angeles Railway 9351, line car
Los Angeles Railway 9550, switcher
Municipal Railway of San Francisco 162, streetcar
Municipal Railway of San Francisco 171, streetcar
Municipal Railway of San Francisco 1039, PCC Car
Pacific Electric 179, center door (b)
Pacific Electric 314 (ex-NWP), interurban
Pacific Electric 418 (ex-IER), interurban
Pacific Electric 498 (ex-IER), interurban
Pacific Electric 331, Birney
Pacific Electric 332, Birney
Pacific Electric 511, interurban (b)
Pacific Electric 538, interurban
Pacific Electric 1000, business car (b)
Pacific Electric 1001, interurban
Pacific Electric 1440, box motor (b)
Pacific Electric 1498, box motor
Pacific Electric 1624, freight motor
Pacific Electric 5112, "Hollywood"
Pacific Electric 5123, "Hollywood"
Pacific Electric 5166, "Hollywood"
Pacific Electric 5167, "Hollywood"
Pacific Electric 00150, trolley greaser
Pacific Electric 00157, line car
Sacramento Northern 653, freight motor
San Diego Electric 88, streetcar (b)
San Diego Electric 93, streetcar (b)
San Diego Electric 167, "Exposition" car (b)
San Diego Electric 508, PCC Car
San Diego Electric 528, PCC Car
San Diego Electric 1003, streetcar (b)
Visalia Electric 301, interurban (b)
Visalia Electric 302, interurban (b)

WESTERN RAILWAY MUSEUM
BAY AREA ELECTRIC RAILROAD ASSN. INC.
RIO VISTA JUNCTION

Central California Traction 7, box motor
Key System 182, articulated unit
Key System 186, articulated unit
Key System 271, streetcar

Key System 352, streetcar
Key System 987, streetcar
Key System 1001, freight motor
Key System 1011, wrecker
Key System 1014, wrecker (b)
Key System 1201, line car
Key System 1215, shop switcher
Key System 1218, line car
Market Street Railway, "San Francisco," private car
Market Street Railway 0109, rail grinder
Market Street Railway 0130, crane
Municipal Railway of San Francisco 178, streetcar
Municipal Railway of San Francisco 1003, streamliner
Municipal Railway of San Francisco 1016, PCC Car
Municipal Railway of San Francisco 1153, PCC Car
Municipal Railway of San Francisco 1190, PCC Car
Municipal Railway of San Francisco C-1, work motor
Napa Valley 63, interurban car
Napa Valley 100, box motor
Pacific Gas and Electric 41, Birney (b)
Pacific Gas and Electric 46, Birney (b)
Peninsular Railway 52, interurban
Peninsular Railway 61, interurban
Petaluma & Santa Rosa 63, interurban
Richmond Shipyard 844, elevated car
Richmond Shipyard 889, elevated car
Sacramento Northern 1, portable substation
Sacramento Northern 62, Birney
Sacramento Northern 602, box motor
Sacramento Northern 652, freight motor
Sacramento Northern 654, freight motor
Sacramento Northern 1005, interurban
Sacramento Northern 1019, interurban
Sacramento Northern 1020, interurban
Sacramento Northern "Bidwell," observation-parlor (a)
San Diego Electric Railway 1043, streetcar
Southern Pacific (Oakland) 332, suburban car
Stockton Electric 56, Birney (b)
Tidewater Southern 200, interurban (b)

(a) Body to be mounted on trucks salvaged from Napa Valley 53, which was destroyed by fire.
(b) Body only, but complete enough that restoration is planned.
   Only cars that are in operating condition or suitable for restoration are included on list, which does not include cars from roads outside California or California cars preserved outside the state.
   —Sources: Bay Area Electric Railroad Association, Peter Hinckley; Orange Empire Railway Museum, Jim Walker.

Ira L. Swett:
An Appreciation

THE PACIFIC ELECTRIC was still a mighty electric railway when Interurbans' founder Ira L. Swett, right, posed in 1948 with fellow railfan and Chicago traction editor George Krambles beside the PE Northern District's finest cars, the big, steel 1100 series, spotted at Sierra Madre. Although the electric railway was an unremarked part of the daily routine of most people when Swett was active, he did not take the traction scene for granted and worked patiently to preserve its history and lore. Swett effortlessly transferred his enthusiasm for his hometown PE and Los Angeles Railway to paper, launching a publishing venture that recorded history and established high editorial standards. Because of Swett, the electric railway has found a firm niche in the history of 20th-century rural and urban America.   *Magna Collection*

ELECTRIC TRACTION RULED SUPREME IN THE Southland when Ira L. Swett was born in 1913 in Los Angeles. The Pacific Electric Railway, the largest interurban railway in the world, was at its zenith, dispatching more than 1,000 trains a day. Equally as impressive was the operation of the narrow-gauged Los Angeles Railway, the yellow streetcar system owned by the Huntington interests. And out in Glendale were the red and white cars of the Glendale & Montrose. One of Swett's cherished memories was seeing Henry Huntington's famous private car, the *Alabama*, rolling through downtown Los Angeles on PE rails. This traction world fascinated Swett and by 1940, when he was 27 years old, he was acknowledged by his peers as being the foremost authority on electric railways in Los Angeles.

Some of Swett's earliest works both in *Interurbans News-Letter* and in Interurbans Specials, and in *Wheel Clicks*, published by Railroad Boosters, carry the byline "Cpl. Ira Swett." He wrote those articles while a member of the United States Army during World War II, and his military career was one reason he entered the publishing field.

Swett was lucky in being stationed close to home during much of the war. Most railfans, however, were assigned to bases far removed from the electric railways they had known as civilians. Swett's early *News-Letters* were intended to tell fans overseas about traction happenings in the United States. Soon he had dozens of readers who also were correspondents, reporting on electric railway activities in the areas where they were assigned.

Swett's wartime duty at the University of Washington at Seattle led to his Specials on Puget Sound Electric and Pacific Northwest Traction. Seattle's trolley buses were brand new upon Swett's arrival and, years later, when it appeared the city would scrap the system, he published his first non-electric railway book, *Seattle Trolley Coaches*, in 1971.

Following World War II, Swett championed modern electric railway technology and offered free copies of *Interurbans* to readers who would use the magazine to promote installation of PCC streetcars in their communities. But electric traction was declining in the United States and Canada and, after printing news of dozens of systems being abandoned, Swett terminated *Interurbans* as a periodic magazine in December 1948. He then concentrated on the histories he issued as "Specials."

Swett wrote about 50 books, with most of his topics being in some way related to the Pacific Electric Railway. Nearly all of his publications used typewritten text and they have an amateur look today. But Swett had little choice; photo typesetting was unheard of during most of Swett's publishing days and hot metal typesetting was far too expensive. Swett's market was limited; if he sold more than 1,500 copies of most of his works he was astonished. So, rather than putting out books that were attractive to the eye but too expensive for many rail history students, Swett published volumes packed with information at a price practically anyone could afford.

And Swett's standards were high, both for himself and the authors he published. At first, Swett published only his own works and, reflecting his never-satisfied curiosity, they were filled with details. One rarely had to ask a question after reading a Special by Swett. That level of detail set a high standard in the electric railway publishing field that most publishers adhere to today.

Readers of Swett's prose often were caught up in the drama of electric railroading, because Swett wrote enthusiastically and colorfully about his topics. Here are his opening words in the Introduction in Special 26:

> The more you think about it, the more the interurban world lost when Sacramento Northern abandoned passenger service. Think it over: One ride—183 miles long, world's longest interurban—brought you more diverse operation than you could buy anywhere else in the U.S.— probably in the world.

A caption under a photograph on Page 76 of Special 16 gave the view of an approaching PE interurban car a certain presence. Swett wrote:

> Where else in western America can you wait in a safety zone and see a behemoth such as this approach?

The March 1946 issue of *Interurbans* carried the news of the approaching abandonment of the Salt Lake & Utah and Swett wrote gently:

> As the time neared for the last car to pull out, old-timers recalled their interesting experiences of the third of a century the Salt Lake & Utah has been operating. Only in their memories will traditions and experiences of the Orem Line's golden years remain. All these, the days when snow stopped the trains, when accidents marred the cars' records, when vaudeville actors hired special trains, and much more occupied their thoughts during the final hours of the SL&U.

Swett's fine writing was no accident. He lived at a time when the written word was an essential of a good education. Also, Ira was not as good a still photographer as some of his contemporaries and this probably was a factor in his books being less dramatic pictorially than they might have been had he been more skilled with a camera, or interested in the medium.

As the years went on, Swett branched out and made some of his color slides and movies available. He formed Interurban Films, which was separated from the book publishing after Swett died in 1975, but returned to Interurban Press in 1985.

An accomplished theater and studio organist, Swett made his living as a musician on early-day radio shows and several of his concerts were recorded. During most of his working career he was a publicist and administrator at the Salvation Army in Los Angeles. His traction books were mostly a hobby and he typically used the revenues from one volume to finance another.

Like many persons who deal with history, Swett knew he was saving something for the future. Swett never married and had no offspring to inherit Interurbans. However, he was intent on continuing the mechanism he so successfully devised to preserve history and made arrangements for Mac Sebree to continue the business, which Sebree and Jim Walker reorganized as Interurban Press. The Glendale-based firm has continued publishing Specials, is in the slide, movie and video business, and owns *Pacific RailNews*, a monthly railfan magazine.

HARRE W. DEMORO

The First 100 Specials

IRA L. SWETT, the founder of what became Interurban Press, began his traction publishing career in April 1943 with the first issue of *Interurbans News-Letter*.

It was his practice—carried to the present by his successors—to issue Special numbers in advance of publishing dates. In a few cases, numbers were later reassigned or not used at all. *I.N.L., The Early Interurban News-letters*, published as X-3 by Interurbans Publications in 1978, contains considerable detail on the early efforts by Swett and reprints many of the early *News-Letters*.

SPECIAL No.	TITLE, AUTHOR AND DATE
1	*The Big Subs*, by Cpl. Ira L. Swett, with Lorin and Ben Silliman, August 1944.
2	*Puget Sound Electric Railway*, by Ira L. Swett, with Harold Hill, Robert S. Wilson, Charles Johnson, Roland Covey and Jim Rice, June 1945.
3	*Pacific Electric All-Time Roster*, by Ira L. Swett, March 1946 (with supplements later).
4	*Bamberger Railroad*, by Ira L. Swett, September 1946.
5	*Denver and Interurban*, by Ira L. Swett, October 1947.
6	*Outstanding Interurban Cars* by Ira L. Swett and Al Barker, August 1948.

SPECIAL No.	TITLE, AUTHOR AND DATE
7	*Pacific Northwest Traction Co.* (North Coast Lines), by Ira L. Swett, with Harold Hill, Lawton Gowey, Robert S. Wilson and Charles Savage, June 1949.
8	*Red Electrics of Portland, Oregon*, by Ira L. Swett, November 1949.
9	*Sacramento Northern* by Ira L. Swett, Arthur L. Lloyd, Vernon J. Sappers, Addison H. Laflin Jr. and Dudley Thickens, June 1950.
10	A news roundup similar to the old monthly magazine but issued as a Special; Ira L. Swett, editor.
11	*Los Angeles Railway* by Ira L. Swett, December 1951.

Bibliography

GENERAL

California, A Guide to the Golden State, Federal Writers' Project of Work Progress Administration, American Guide Series, May 1939, revised 1954, Harry Hansen, ed., Hastings House, New York, 1973.

Coleman, Charles, *PG&E of California*, McGraw-Hill, New York, 1952.

Cox, Harold E., *The Birney Car*, Harold Eugene Cox, Forty Fort, Pa., 1966.

Hilton, George W. and John F. Due, *The Electric Interurban Railways in America*, Stanford, 1960.

Johnston, Hank, *The Railroad That Lighted Southern California*, Trans-Anglo, Los Angeles, 1965.

Lind, Alan R., *From Horsecars to Streamliners*, Transport History Press, Forest Park, Ill., 1978.

Middleton, William D., *The Interurban Era*, Kalmbach, Milwaukee, 1961.

_____ *The Time of the Trolley*, Kalmbach, Milwaukee, 1967.

_____ *When the Steam Railroads Electrified*, Kalmbach, Milwaukee, 1974.

_____ *Traction Classics*, I and II, Golden West, San Marino, 1983 and 1985.

Miller, John Anderson, *Fares Please!* D. Appleton-Century, New York, 1941.

Myers, William A., *Iron Men and Copper Wires*, Trans-Anglo, Glendale, 1984.

Narell, Irena, *Our City, The Jews of San Francisco*, Howell-North, San Diego, 1981.

Young, Andrew and Eugene F. Provenzo Jr., *A History of the St. Louis Car Co.*, Howell-North, Berkeley, 1978.

"Electric Railroading in Central California," *Pacific Railway Journal*, Vol. 1, No. 12, December 1956.

"First Century," *Southern Pacific Bulletin*, August 1955.

"Around San Francisco Bay," by Harre W. Demoro, *The Bulletin*, National Railway Historical Society, Vol. 35, No. 2, Philadelphia, 1970.

McGraw Electric Railway Directory, McGraw Hill, New York, 1931.

"California and Her Tractions," reprint of 1920 *Electric Railway Journal* articles, *Traction Heritage*, Vol. 4, No. 1, Indianapolis, January 1971.

Interurbans Specials 6, 24, 64, 85, 86, 91.

BAKERSFIELD

"Bakersfield & Kern Electric Railway," *The Western Railroader*, February 1955, Vol. 18, No. 4, Issue 184.

EUREKA

"Street Railways of Eureka," by Stanley T. Borden, *The Western Railroader*, Vol. 27, No. 10, Issue 297, October 1964.

FRESNO

"Fresno Traction and Fresno Interurban," by Steve Renovich, *The Western Railroader*, August 1960, Vol. 23, No. 8, Issue 248.

Interurbans Special 73.

LOS ANGELES

Crump, Spencer, *Ride the Big Red Cars*, Trans-Anglo, Corona del Mar, 1977.

_____ *Henry Huntington and the Pacific Electric*, Trans-Anglo, Corona del Mar, 1970.

Duke, Donald, ed., *Pacific Electric*, Pacific Railway Journal, San Marino, 1958.

Easlon, Steven L., *The Los Angeles Railway Through the Years*, Darwin, Sherman Oaks, 1973.

Howard, Danny, ed., *Southern California and the Pacific Electric*, Daniel L. Howard, Los Angeles, 1980.

Moreau, Jeffrey and James Walker Jr., *Glendale & Montrose*, Pacific Bookwork, Los Angeles, 1966.

Moreau, Jeffrey, ed., *The Pacific Electric Pictorial*, Pacific Bookwork, Los Angeles, 1964.

Seims, Charles, *Mount Lowe, The Railway in the Clouds*, Golden West, San Marino, 1976.

"PE Red Cars Remembered," by Harre W. Demoro, *Pacific News*, Vol. 19, No. 4, Issue 210, April 1979.

Interurbans Specials 3, 11, 12, 13, 16, 18, 20, 21, 27, 28, 30, 33, 35, 36, 37, 38, 39, 40, 41, 43, 46, 48, 60, 61, 63, 92.

San Francisco-Oakland-Marin

"Municipal Railway, 1912-1944," by Waldemar Sievers, *The Western Railroader*, Issues 260, 311, 335, 338 and 341 combined into undated Booklet 260-SS.

"San Francisco Municipal Railway, 1944-1964," Laflin, Addison, John E. Perry Jr., and Robert Townley, *The Western Railroader*, issued as Booklet 286-E, no date.

"Market Street Railway, 1934-1944," *The Western Railroader*, 258, 267, 264, issued as undated Booklet 258-S.

"The 40 Line," *The Western Railroader*, incorporating Issues 111, 185, 326 in undated Booklet 111-E (revised).

"San Francisco & San Mateo Electric Railway," *The Western Railroader*, Vol. 38, Issue 417, March 1975.

"San Mateo Line, The Big Subs," *The Western Railroader*, Vol. 38, Issue 422, August 1975.

"San Francisco to the 40-Line Cemeteries," *The Western Railroader and Western Railfan*, Vol. 39, Issue 427, January 1976.

"The 40 Line," *The Western Railroader and Western Railfan*, Vol. 39, Issue 433, July 1976.

"South San Francisco Railroad & Power Co.," *The Western Railroader and Western Railfan*, Vol. 40, Issue 438.

"IER, The Big Red Cars," *The Western Railroader*, Issues 199 and 318 combined into undated booklet.

A History of the Key Decisions in the Development of Bay Area Rapid Transit, BART Impact Program, U.S. Department of Transportation, Metropolitan Transportation Commission, Document FR 3-14-75, McDonald & Smart Inc., September 1975.

Transit Times, special issue on Oakland area transit history, Alameda-Contra Costa Transit District, Vol. 6, No. 5, September 1963.

"East Bay Transit," *The Western Railroader*, Vol. 36, Issue 397, May 1973.

"Key System Interurban Lines," *The Western Railroader*, Issue 384, February 1972 and others combined into Booklet 384-E.

Strapac, Joseph, *BART Off & Running*, Chatham, Burlingame, 1972.

"BART Is Off and Running," by Harre W. Demoro, *The Bulletin*, National Railway Historical Society, Vol. 37, No. 6, 1972.

"The BART Experience, What Have We Learned?" by Melvin M. Webber, Monograph 26, Institute of Urban and Regional Development and Institute of Transportation Studies, University of California, Berkeley, October 1976.

"A Documented Account of the Conversion from Rail Service to Motor Bus by the Key System," by Harre W. Demoro, *National Railway Bulletin*, Vol. 44, No. 6, National Railway Historical Society, 1979.

"Shipyard Railway," by Harre W. Demoro, *Pacific News*, Vol. 17, No. 11, Issue 193, November 1977.

"Key System Remembered," by Harre W. Demoro, *Pacific News*, Vol. 18, No. 13, Issue 197, March 1978.

Hanson, Erle C., "East Shore & Suburban Railway," *Pacific Railway Journal*, San Marino, 1961.

"Interurban Lines Northwestern Pacific." by Waldemar Sievers, *The Western Railroader*, incorporating Issues 178 (August 1954), 308 (September 1965) and others in booklet with 1904 *Street Railway Journal* article.

"Ocean Shore Railroad, Reaches the Beaches," by Rudolph Brandt, *The Western Railroader*, Vol. 15, No. 7, Issue 151, no date.

Trimble, Paul C., *Interurban Railways of the Bay Area*, Valley Publishers, Fresno, 1977.

Wagner, Jack R., *The Last Whistle*, Howell-North, Berkeley, 1974.

Interurban Specials 1, 31, 44, 56, 65, 68, 69, 75, 79, 84, 89, 95, 97.

San Diego

Dodge, Richard V., "Rails of the Silver Gate," *Pacific Railway Journal*, San Marino, 1960.

Hanft, Robert M., *San Diego & Arizona, the Impossible Railroad*, Trans-Anglo, Glendale, 1984.

Sacramento

"Street Railways of Sacramento," *The Western Railroader*, Vol. 19, No. 12, Issue 204, October 1956.

"Streetcars of Sacramento," map of system in 1920s, Blymyer No. 2, January 1984.

Interurbans Specials 9, 26, 32, 34.

San Jose

"Peninsular Issue," by Cpl. Ira L. Swett, Ralph Melching, ed., *Wheel Clicks*, Vol. 5, No. 1, July 1944, Railroad Boosters, Los Angeles.

"Peninsular Railway Co., Blossom Line," incorporating Issues 348 (February 1969), 352 (June 1969), 355 (October 1969) and other material, *The Western Railroader*, booklet 348-E, 1969.

"Streetcars in Palo Alto," *The Western Railroader*, Vol. 14, No. 10, Issue 142, August 1951.

"San Jose Railroads," by Henry Morse, *The Western Railroader*, Booklet 373-E.

Interurbans Special 78.

SANTA BARBARA

"Santa Barbara & Suburban Railway," by William Everett, *The Western Railroader*, Vol. 16, No. 9, Issue 165, July 1953, from *O-Gauge Modeler*, February 1953.

Everett, William B. and Gary B. Coombs, *Mule Car and Trolley*, Institute for American Research, Goleta, Calif., 1984.

SANTA CRUZ

"Union Traction of Santa Cruz," *The Western Railroader and Western Railfan*, Vol. 4, Issue 444, July 1977.

Interurbans Special 67.

STOCKTON

"Stockton Electric Railway," *The Western Railroader*, Vol. 20, No. 6, Issue 210, April 1957.

CENTRAL COAST

"Monterey & Pacific Grove Street Railway," by Erle C. Hanson, *The Western Railroader*, Vol. 22, No. 10, Issue 238, September 1959.

"Watsonville Transportation Co.," by H.W. Fabing, *The Western Railroader*, Vol. 29, No. 11, Issue 322, November 1966.

Best, Gerald M., *Ships and Narrow Gauge Rails, The Story of the Pacific Coast Co.*, Howell-North, Berkeley, 1964.

INTERURBAN LINES

"Petaluma & Santa Rosa Electric Railroad," by Stanley T. Borden, *The Western Railroader*, Vol. 23, No. 4, Issue 244, April 1960.

"Tidewater Southern Railway," *The Western Railroader*, Vol. 13, No. 11, Issue 131, September 1950.

"Sacramento Northern," *The Western Railroader*, Vol. 13, No. 8, Issue 128, June 1950.

"Sacramento Northern Oroville Branch," *The Western Railroader*, Vol. 43, No. 476, May-June 1980.

"End of an Era, 25 Years on Sacramento Northern," *The Western Railroader*, Vol. 27, No. 7, Issue 294, July 1964.

"Oakland, Antioch & Eastern Railway," reproduction of article in October 1913 *Electric Journal* in *The Western Railroader*, Vol. 34, No. 12, Issue 382, December 1971.

"The Vallejo & Northern and Other Electric Railroads of Solano County," by Addison H. Laflin Jr., *The Western Railroader*, Vol. 16, No. 2, Issue 158, December 1952.

"Visalia Electric Railroad," by Steven B. Renovich, *The Western Railroader*, Vol. 22, No. 8, Issue 236, June 1959.

"Napa Valley Route," *The Western Railroader*, incorporating Issue 160 (February 1953) and other material into undated Booklet 160-E.

"Sacramento Northern," by Harre W. Demoro, *The Bulletin*, National Railway Historical Society, Vol. 37, No. 6, 1972.

For Nevada County Traction (Grass Valley-Nevada City) see Best, Gerald M., *Nevada County Narrow Gauge*, Howell-North, Berkeley, 1965, and "Nevada County Traction Co.," *The Western Railroader*, Vol. 13, No. 8, Issue 122, December 1949.

For San Francisco & Napa Valley, see Interurbans Special 47.

For Sacramento Northern, see Interurbans Specials 9, 26, 32, 34.

Index

Other Books by Harre W. Demoro: